CHAPMAN & HALL/CRC THE PYTHON SERIES

About the Series

Python has been ranked as the most popular programming language, and it is widely used in education and industry. This book series will offer a wide range of books on Python for students and professionals. Titles in the series will help users learn the language at an introductory and advanced level, and explore its many applications in data science, AI, and machine learning. Series titles can also be supplemented with Jupyter notebooks.

For more information about this series please visit: www.crcpress.com/ Chapman – HallCRC/book-series/PYTH

Learning Professional Python

Python

Volume 1: The Basics

Usharani Bhimavarapu
and Jude D. Hemanth

CRC Press
Taylor & Francis Group
Boca Raton London New York

CRC Press is an imprint of the
Taylor & Francis Group, an **informa** business

A CHAPMAN & HALL BOOK

Cover Image Credit: Shutterstock.com

First edition published 2024
by CRC Press
2385 NW Executive Center Drive, Suite 320, Boca Raton, FL 33431

and by CRC Press
4 Park Square, Milton Park, Abingdon, Oxon, OX14 4RN

CRC Press is an imprint of Taylor & Francis Group, LLC

© 2024 Usharani Bhimavarapu and Jude D. Hemanth

Library of Congress Cataloging-in-Publication Data
Names: Bhimavarapu, Usharani, author. | Hemanth, D. Jude, author.
Title: Learning professional Python / Usharani Bhimavarapu, D. Jude Hemanth.
Description: First edition. | Boca Raton : CRC Press, 2024. | Includes
    bibliographical references and index.
Identifiers: LCCN 2023007977 | ISBN 9781032539256 (volume 1 ; hbk) |
    ISBN 9781032534237 (volume 1 ; pbk) | ISBN 9781003414322
    (volume 1 ; ebk) | ISBN 9781032611761 (volume 2 ; hbk) | ISBN
    9781032611709 (volume 2 ; pbk) | ISBN 9781003462392 (volume 2 ; ebk)
Subjects: LCSH: Python (Computer program language) | Computer
    programming.
Classification: LCC QA76.73.P98 B485 2024 | DDC 005.13/3—dc23/eng/
    20230508
LC record available at https://lccn.loc.gov/2023007977

ISBN: 978-1-032-53925-6 (hbk)
ISBN: 978-1-032-53423-7 (pbk)
ISBN: 978-1-003-41432-2 (ebk)

DOI: 10.1201/9781003414322

Typeset in Minion
by Apex CoVantage, LLC

Contents

Preface

Python is a general-purpose interpreted programming language used for deep learning, machine learning, and complex data analysis. Python is a perfect language for beginners as it is easy to learn and understand. This book is intended to teach the reader how to program in Python. The book aims to get you up to speed fast enough and have you writing real Python programs in no time at all. It assumes no previous exposure to the Python language and is suited to both beginners and experienced programmers. This book gives a comprehensive, in-depth introduction to the core Python language.

This book helps you in gaining a quick grasp of the fundamentals of Python programming and working with built-in functions. The book then moves to help you in exception handling, data wrangling, databases with Python, regular expressions, NumPy arrays, data frames and plotting. The Python Programming culminates with how you can continue learning Python after reading this book and leaves you with a problem to solve, testing your skills even at the last step.

The book contains approximately 500 tested programs, and all these programs have been tested using the IDE Anaconda, Google colaboratory, and Python online compilers compatible to the Windows operating system and discussed the appropriate nature of the output. The book further mentions a summary of the technical aspects of interviewing tips on negotiating the best offer and guiding the best way.

This book is for data analysts, IT developers, and anyone looking to get started with or transition to the field of software or refresh their knowledge of Python programming. This book will also be useful for students planning to build a career in data engineering or IT professionals preparing for a transition. No previous knowledge of data engineering is required. The book aims to get you up to speed fast enough and have you writing real Python programs in no time at all.

It contains 12 chapters, and at the end of every chapter, practice exercises are given to enable the learners to review the knowledge gained. Each chapter starts with a brief introduction, top tips, and a review of the essential library methods, finally followed by broad and thought-provoking problems.

We are thankful to Taylor and Francis Publications for undertaking the publication of this book and supporting us in this endeavor. Any suggestions for the improvement of the book will be thankfully acknowledged and incorporated in the next edition.

Dr. Usharani Bhimavarapu
Dr. Jude D. Hemanth

Author Biographies

Usharani Bhimavarapu is working as an assistant professor in the Computer Science and Engineering Department at Koneru Lakshmaiah Education Foundation at Vaddeswaram, Andhra Pradesh, India. She has been teaching for the last 14 years with emphasis on data mining, machine learning, and data structure. She communicated more than 40 research papers in SCI, SCIE, and Scopus indexed journals. She has authored 12 books in programming languages like CPP, Java, Python, HTML, CSS, and so on.

Dr. Jude D. Hemanth received his BE degree in ECE from Bharathiar University in 2002, ME degree in communication systems from Anna University in 2006, and PhD from Karunya University in 2013. His research areas include computational intelligence and image processing. He has authored more than 230 research papers in reputed SCIE indexed international journals and Scopus indexed international conferences. His cumulative impact factor is more than 350. He has published 37 edited books with reputed publishers such as Elsevier, Springer, and IET.

He has been serving as an associate editor of SCIE indexed international journals such as *IEEE Journal of Biomedical and Health Informatics* (IEEE-JBHI), *IEEE Transactions on Intelligent Transportation Systems*, *Soft Computing* (Springer), *Earth Science Informatics* (Springer), *IET Image Processing*, *Heliyon* (Elsevier), *Mathematical Problems in Engineering*, *PeerJ Computer Science*, *PLOS One*, and *Dyna* (Spain). He also holds the associate editor/guest editor position with many Scopus journals. He has been serving as the series editor of Biomedical Engineering series (Elsevier), editorial board member of ASTI series (Springer), and Robotics and Healthcare series (CRC Press).

He has received a project grant of 35,000 UK pounds from the UK government (GCRF scheme) with collaborators from the University of Westminster, UK. He has also completed two funded research projects from CSIR and DST, the government of India. He also serves as the research scientist of Computational Intelligence and Information Systems (CI2S) Lab, Argentina; LAPISCO Research Lab, Brazil; RIADI Lab, Tunisia; Research Centre for Applied Intelligence, University of Craiova, Romania; and eHealth and Telemedicine Group, University of Valladolid, Spain.

He is the NVIDIA university ambassador and NVIDIA certified instructor for deep learning courses. His name was featured in the "Top 2% Leading World Scientists" [2021, 2022] list released by Stanford University, USA. He is an international accreditation member for higher education institutions in Romania [ARACIS] and Slovenia [SQAA] under the European Commission. Currently, he is working as a professor in the Department of ECE, Karunya University, Coimbatore, India.

## CHAPTER 1

Python Basics

$\mathbf{P}$ython is a regular general-purpose, high-level, and object-oriented programming language. Python is an interpreted scripting language. Python is a simple-to-understand and multipurpose scripting language. Python is a multipurpose programming language. It can be used with web, enterprise applications. Python makes the development and the debugging fast.

1.1 HISTORY OF PYTHON

Python was created by Guido Van Rossum in the early nineteenth century at the national research institute for mathematics and computer science in the Netherlands. Python is obtained from several additional programming languages like ABC, Modula-3, C, CPP, Smalltalk, Unix, and scripting languages. Python is accessible under the GNU public license (GPU)

1.2 ADVANTAGES OF PYTHON

1. Python is interpreted – There is no need to compile the python program before executing it.

2. Python is interactive – The developer can relate to the interpreter immediately to write the python programs.

3. Python is object oriented – Python maintains an object-oriented programming concept that encapsulates the code contained by objects.

1.3 CHARACTERISTICS OF PYTHON

The important characteristics of Python programming:

1. Python provides a high-level dynamic data type and strengthens dynamic type checking.

2. Python is opensource; it can contribute to the development code.

3. Python is as understandable as plain English.

4. Python supports functional, structure, as well as object-oriented programming methods.

5. Python supports automatic garbage collection.

6. Python source code can be converted to the byte code.

7. Easy to learn – Python has a straightforward structure and obviously defined syntax. It is simple to read, easy to provide, and cross-platform compatible.

8. Easy to teach – Workload is smaller when compared to other programming languages techniques.

9. Easy to use – Python code is faster than other programming languages.

10. Easy to understand – Easier to understand than other programming languages.

11. Easy to obtain – Python is free, open source, and multiplatform.

1.4 APPLICATIONS OF PYTHON

1. Portable – Python can run on all platforms, like Unix, Windows, and Macintosh.

2. Extendable – The developer can combine low-level modules to the Python interpreter. These modules allow the programmers to modify their tools useful database.

3. Python offers interface to the commercial databases.

4. GUI programming – Python encourages graphical user interface applications by system calls, libraries, and Windows systems such as Windows MFC Macintosh and the X Windows system of Unix.

5. Scalable – Python offers systematic structure and assist shell scripting.

1.5 PYTHON VERSIONS

1. CPython

2. Cython

3. Jython

4. PyPy

5. RPython

1.6 PYTHON IDENTIFIERS

A Python identifier is their name used to recognize a variable, function, module, class, or an object. An identifier begins with the letter, or an underscore followed by digits. Python does not permit punctuation marks such as @, $, ^. Python is a case-sensitive programming language. For example, Test and test are two unique identifiers in Python.

Naming rules for Python identifiers:

1. Class names begin with an uppercase letter. All additional identifiers beginning with a lowercase letter.

2. If the identifier closes with two trailing underscores, the identifier is the language specified special name.

3. Beginning with an identifier with a particular leading _underscore signifies that the identifier is private.

4. Beginning an identifier with the two prominent underscores indicates it is an intensely private identifier.

1.7 RESERVED WORDS

Table 1.1 shows the Python keywords. These keywords cannot be used as a constant or variable or any other identifier names.

TABLE 1.1   Reserve Words

and	exec	not
assert	finally	or
break	for	pass
class	from	print
continue	global	raise
def	if	return
del	import	try
elif	in	while
else	Is	with
except	lambda	yield

1.8 PRINT () FUNCTION

The print () prints a message onto the screen or to the standard output.

Syntax

```
print (object, sep=separator, end=end, file= file,
flush=flush)
```

- sep – Specifies the separator between the outputted argument.
- end – Specifies what to print at the end of the print statement
- flush – Flushes the screen. Its default value is false
- file – Where to display the message object. The default out is to the console, that is, std.out. The programmers can output the message to the file also.

The end and sep are the keyword arguments, and these parameters are used to format the output of the print () function. The programmers can enter more than one object separated by separator. An empty print () outputs an empty line to the screen.

Your first python program:

```
print ("this is to test")
```

The previous line produces the output:

```
this is to test
```

If we remove double quotes in the print statement:

```
print(this is to test)
```

Output

```
File "<ipython-input-86-c0dae74495e9>", line 1
print(this is to test)
                 ^
SyntaxError: invalid syntax
```

print () can operate with all types of data provided by Python. The data type data strings, numbers, characters, objects, logical values can be successfully passed to print ().

 NOTE: print () does not evaluate anything.

Program

```
print("this is to test")
print("this is the second line in python program")
```

Output

```
this is to test
this is the second line in python program
```

The preceding program invokes the print () twice. The print () begins its output from a fresh new line each time it starts its execution. The output of the code is produced in the same order in which they have been placed in the source file. The first line in the preceding program produces the output [this is to test], and the second line produces the output [this is the second line in python program]. The empty print () with without any arguments produces the empty line, that is, just a new empty line.

Program

```
print("this is to test")
print()
print("this is the second line in python program")
```

Output

```
this is to test
this is the second line in python program
```

In the preceding program, the second line print statement introduces the empty line.

The following programs illustrate the separator and end argument:

Program

```
print("this","is","to","test",end="@")
```

Output

```
this is to test@
```

In the preceding program, end separator is used, so after printing the string, the separator has been added.

Program

```
print("this is"," to test",sep="---",end="#")
print("this is an experiment")
```

Output

```
this is--- to test#this is an experiment
```

The string assigned to the end keyword argument can be any length. The sep arguments value may be an empty string. In the previous example, the separator is specified as –. The first and the second argument is separated by the separator. In the preceding program the separator is –. So the output is [this is – to test]. In the first the print statement, the end argument specified is "#". So after printing the first print statement, the # symbol is placed, the first line output is [this is – to test#].

Program

```
print("this","is","to","test",end="\n\n\n")
print("this is an experiment")
```

Output

```
this is to test
this is an experiment
```

In the preceding program, "\n" is used as the end separator, so after printing the first line string, new lines have been added.

1.9 LINES AND INDENTATION

The Python statement does not end with a semicolon. Python gives no braces to specify blocks of code for class and function definitions or flow control. Blocks of code are represented by line indentation. The number of spaces in the indentation is valuable, and the old statements within the block must be invented the same indentation. In Python, all the continuous lines are indented with the equivalent number of spaces, which would form a block. For example:

```
def test():
a=1
print(a)
```

The preceding program produces the output 1.

1.10 MULTILINE STATEMENTS

Statements in Python predictably end with the new line. Python permits use of the line continuation character to denote that the line should continue.

```
a=test_one+\
test_two+\
test_three
```

Statements continued with [], {}, () do not need to use the line continuation character, for example:

```
a= {1,2,3,4,
5,6,7}
```

1.11 QUOTATION IN PYTHON

Python allows single, double, and triple quotes to signify string literals. The triple quotes are applied to spend the string within multiple lines. For example, the following are legal:

```
S="test"
S='test'
S=""" This is to test a multiple lines and sentence """
```

1.12 COMMENTS IN PYTHON

A hash sign (#) is the starting of the comment. All characters after the hash and up to the end of the line are part of the comment, and the Python interpreter ignores that line. For example:

   print ("this is to test") # Python comment

   The Python developer can comment multiple lines as follows:

```
#This is the first comment
#this is the second line comment
#This is the third line comment
#this is also a comment
```

Note: Comments omitted at runtime and these comments leave additional information in code.

Note: The triple quoted string is also ignored by Python interpreter and can be used as a multiline comment.

```
'''this is the
test the
multiline comment '''',
```

Program

```
print("test#1")
print("test#2")
#print("test#3)
```

Output

```
test#1
test#2
```

In the preceding program, the first and the second print statement consists of the # statement in between the quotes, so this # symbol behaves like a symbol, and the interpreter prints that symbol. But at line 3 the # symbol is in front of print statement. In this case # symbol works as comment.

Program

```
#this is
to test comment
print("python comment")
```

Output

```
File "<ipython-input-28-b77848f8c85d>", line 2
to test comment
     ^
SyntaxError: invalid syntax
```

If we want to display anything at runtime, we must put that content in quotes inside print statement, otherwise the interpreter throws the error. In the preceding program, the second line consists of the string without the print statement. So this line throws the error.

1.13 MULTIPLE STATEMENTS ON A SINGLE LINE

The semicolon (;) lets multiple statements on the single and given that neither statement starts in new code block. For example:

```
x='test';print(x)
```

Output

```
test
```

1.14 PYTHON VARIABLES

Every variable has a name and a value. Variables are used to store values stop. That means when the developer creates a variable, the translator allocates memory and decides what can be saved in the reserved memory. By allocating different data types of variables, you can store integers, decimals, or characters in these variables.

Syntax

```
variable name=value
E.g.: i=100
```

Note: If the programmer assigns any value to a nonexistent variable, the variable will be automatically created, that is, a variable comes into existence because of allocating a value to the variable.

1.15 NAMING CONVENTIONS TO VARIABLES

1. The name of the variables must be composed of uppercase or lowercase alphabets (A . . . Z, a . . . z), digits (0 . . . 9) and the special symbol underscore (_).

2. The name of the variable must begin with a letter or the special symbol underscore (_) but not with a digit.

3. The name of the variables must be a reserved keyword.

4. Uppercase and lowercase letters are treated as different in Python.

5. Python does not have any restrictions on the length of the variable name.

6. Some valid variable names are test, sum, test_sum, test1, test1_avg, myVariable.

7. Some invalid variable names are 5sum, test sum, False, None.

Note: Python is a dynamically typed language; no need to declare the type of the variable.

1.16 ASSIGNING VALUES TO VARIABLES

Python variables do not require specific declaration to reserve memory space. The declaration occurs automatically when you allocate a value to your variable. The = is applied to allocate values to variables. The operating to the left of the = to operator is the name of the variable and the operand to the right of the = operator is the value stored in the variable. For example:

```
t=100
sname='rani'
```

In the previous example, t and the sname are the variable names and 100 and 'rani' are the variable values.

Note: The programmer can assign a new value to the already existing variable by using either the assignment operator or the shortcut operator.

Program

```
Test=1
print(test)
```

Output

```
---------------------------------------------------------------
NameError                    Traceback (most recent call last)
<ipython-input-23-f210fd97eab0> in <module>()
1 Test=1
----> 2 print(test)
NameError: name 'test' is not defined
```

Name error has occurred because the variable name is Test but in print the variable name is test.

Program

```
i=100
i=50+500
print(i)
```

Output

```
550
```

In the previous example, variable i is assigned an integer literal 100, and in the second line the value of i is reassigned to 550(50 + 500). The variable retains its latest value, that is, in the second line the old value (i.e., 100) is overwritten by the value 550(50 + 500).

Program

```
a='5'
b="5"
print(a+b)
```

Output

```
55
```

In the preceding program, the value of a is character literal 5 but not the numeric value. The value of b is string literal 5. The third line performs the computation a+b. Here + works as the concatenation operator.

Program: Find the hypotheses of the triangle

```
a=5.0
b=3.0
c=(a**2+b**2)**0.5
print("c=",c)
```

Output

```
c= 5.830951894845301
```

In the preceding program, the ** is the exponentiation operator. In line 3, during expression evaluation, interpreter first computes the expression a**2+b**2, the higher priority gives to the parenthesis's operator.

1.17 MULTIPLE ASSIGNMENT

Python allows to allocate a single value to several variables simultaneously. For example:

```
a=b=c=1
```

In the previous line, the value of a, b, and c is 1.

```
a, b, c=1,2,3
```

In the previous example the value a is 1, b is 2, and c is 3.

1.18 NONE VARIABLE

None is a keyword in python, and this word used in circumstances

1. To assign to a variable

   E.g., test=None

2. To compare with another variable

   if(test==None):

   if test is None:

Scope of the variables in Python

1. Global

2. Local

1.19 DATA TYPES

The data stored in memory off many types. Python has various standard data types, like numbers, strings, list, tuple, dictionary. Number data types store numeric values, for example Var1= 1.

Python supports four different numeric types:

- int
- long
- float
- complex

1.20 TYPE CONVERSION

Python supports several built-in functions to complete conversion from one data type to another data type. These functions restore the converted values. Python supports 2 types of data conversions

1. Implicit conversion

2. Explicit conversion

1.20.1 Implicit Conversion

Python automatically converts one data type to another data type. There is no need for user involvement.

Program: Implicit Conversion

```
x=123
y=12.34
print(x+y)
x=123
y=10.0
print(x+y)
x=10+1j
y=10.0
print(x+y)
```

Output

```
135.34
133.0
(20+1j)
```

Program: Implicit Conversion

```
x="test"
y=10
print(x+y)
```

Output

```
----------------------------------------------------------------
TypeError                                              Traceback
(most recent call last)
```

```
<ipython-input-65-d2c36b20b8bd> in <module>()
1 x="test"
2 y=10
----> 3 print(x+y)
TypeError: can only concatenate str (not "int") to str
```

1.20.2 Explicit Conversion

In explicit type conversion, the programmers must use the predefined functions. This type of conversion is also known as the type casting because the users are forcing the one data type to another data type by using predefined functions. The following table gives some predefined explicit type conversion functions.

TABLE: Conversion Function

Conversion Function	Description
int (x [, base])	Converts x to an integer and x is a string
long (x [, base])	Converts x to a long and x is a string
float(x)	Converts x to a floating-point number
complex (real [, imag])	Creates a complex number
tuple(x)	Converts x to tuple
set(x)	Converts x to set
list(x)	Converts x to list
dict(d)	Creates a dictionary
chr(x)	Converts an integer to character
hex(x)	Converts an integer to hexadecimal value
oct(x)	Converts an integer to octal value

Program

```
x="1010"
print("string=",x)
print("conversion to int=",int(x,2))
print("conversion to float=",float(x))
print("conversion to complex=",complex(x))
x=10
print("converting to hexadecimal=",hex(x))
print("converting to octal=",oct(x))
print("conversion to Ascii=",chr(x))
x='test'
print("conversion to tuple=",tuple(x))
print("conversion to set=",set(x))
```

Output

```
string= 1010
conversion to int= 10
conversion to float= 1010.0
conversion to complex= (1010+0j)
converting to hexadecimal= 0xa
converting to octal= 0o12
conversion to Ascii=
conversion to tuple= ('t', 'e', 's', 't')
conversion to set= {'s', 't', 'e'}
```

The preceding program uses the explicit data type conversion.

1.21 LITERALS

Literals are nothing but some fixed values in code. Python has various types of literals – number (e.g., 111 or – 1), float literal (e.g., 2.5 or – 2.5), string literal (e.g., 'test' or "test"), Boolean literal (True/False), None literal.

Note: None literal is used to signify the absence of a value.

Note: Python 3.6 introduced versions of underscores in numeric literals. For example, 11_11.

Note: Python print () function automatically does the conversion to the decimal representation from other number systems.

Note: Python omits zero when it is the only digit in front or after the decimal point.

In Python the number 1 is an integer literal and 1.0 is the float literal.

The programmer has to input the value 1.0 as 1. and 0.1 as .1. To avoid writing many zeros in, Python uses the scientific notation E or e. For example, 10000000 can be represented as 1E7 or 1e7. The value before the e is the base, and the value after the e is the exponent. For example, the float literal 0.000000001 can be represented as 1e-9 or 1E-9.

1.22 BINARY NUMBER SYSTEM

A binary number system is expressed in zeros and ones.

Program

```
print(0o13)#octal representation
print(0x13)#hexadecimal representation
```

Output

```
11
19
```

EXERCISE

1. Write the first line of code in the python program using the sep= "$" and

   end= " . . . " keywords.

   print ("this", "is", "to", 'test")

   print ("python language")

2. Write the first line of code in the python program using the sep= "***" and end= "----" keywords.

   print ("this", "is", "to", "test")

   print ("python language")

3. Write the first line of code in the python program using the sep= "*" and end= "\n" keywords and second line of code using the sep= "#" and end= "---".

   print ("this", "is", "to", "test")

   print ("python language")

4. Check the following code:

   print (true>false)

   print (true<false)

5. What is the decimal value for the binary number 1101?

6. What is the decimal value for the binary number 1001?

7. What is the hexadecimal value for the binary number 1101?

8. What is the octal value for the binary number 1101?

9. What is the octal value for the decimal number 145?

10. What is the hexadecimal value for the decimal number 123?

## CHAPTER 2

Python Operators

2.1 OPERATORS INTRODUCTION

An operator is a symbol that can operate on the operands. The operators can be classified as follows:

1. Unary Operator

2. Binary Operator

3. Ternary Operator

2.1.1 Unary Operators

It works on single variable. The unary operators in python are the following:

+, −,

2.1.2 Binary Operator

It works on single variables. For binary operators, refer to section 2.2.

2.1.3 Ternary Operator

It works on three variables. Ternary operator evaluates the expression based on the condition being true or false. Ternary operator allows the testing condition in a single line instead of the multiline if else code.

DOI: 10.1201/9781003414322-2

```
a,b = 10, 20
print(a if a> b else b)
```

Output

```
20
```

2.2 BINARY OPERATORS

Python language supports the seven types of binary operators:

1. Arithmetic Operators

2. Relational Operators

3. Assignment Operators

4. Logical Operators

5. Bitwise Operators

6. Membership Operators

7. Identity Operators

2.2.1 Arithmetic Operators

TABLE   Arithmetic Operators

S.No	Operator	Name	Example	Program	Result
1	+	addition	a+b	a,b=1,4 print(a+b)	5
2	−	subtraction	a-b	a,b=10,5 print(a-b)	5
3	*	multiplication	a*b	a,b=10,5 print(a*b)	50
4	/	division	a/b	a,b=10,3 print(a/b)	3.3333333333333335
5	%	modulus	a%b	a,b=10,3 print(a%b)	1
6	**	exponentiation	a**b	a,b=10,5 print(a**b)	100000
7	//	floor division	a//b	a,b=10,3 print(a//b)	3

Program

```
Python 3.6.2 Shell                                                    —    □    ×

File  Edit  Shell  Debug  Options  Window  Help
Python 3.6.2 (v3.6.2:5fd33b5, Jul  8 2017, 04:14:34) [MSC v.1900 32 bit (Intel)]
on win32
Type "copyright", "credits" or "license()" for more information.
>>> a=10
>>> b=4
>>> a+b
14
>>> a-b
6
>>> a*b
40
>>> a/b
2.5
>>> a%b
2
>>> a**b
10000
>>> a//b
2
>>> (a%b)+a**b-(a*b)/(a//b)
9982.0
>>> |
                                                              Ln: 21  Col: 4
```

The preceding program is about Python program to perform arithmetic operations.

Note: For **(exponentiation) operator the left argument is the base, and the right argument is the exponent (base^{exponent} e.g.: $2**3 = 2^3 = 8$).

Note: When using **, if both operands are integers, then the result is an integer.

Note: When using **, if one of the operands is float, then the result is a float.

Note: The result produced by the division operator is always a float value.

Note: For integer divisional operator (//), the result is always rounded towards the lesser integer value.

Note: When using //, if both operands are integers, then the result is an integer.

Note: When using //, if one of the operands is float, then the result is a float.

2.2.2 Shortened Operators

TABLE   Assignment Operators (Screenshot)

S.No	Operator	Name	Example	Program	Result
1	=	assignment	a=b	a,b= 10,5	
2	+=	add and	a+=b	a,b=10,5 a+=b print(a)	15
3	−=	subtract and	a-=b	a,b=10,5 a-=b print(a)	5
4	*=	multiply and	a*=b	a,b=10,5 a*=b print(a)	50
5	/=	divide and	a/=b	a,b=10,5 a/=b print(a)	2.0
6	%=	modulus and	a%=b	a,b=10,5 a%=b print(a)	0
7	//=	floor division and	a//=b	a,b=10,5 a//=b print(a)	2
8	**=	exponent and	a**=b	a,b=10,5 a**=b print(a)	100000
9	&=	bitwise and	a&=b	a,b=10,5 a&=b print(a)	0

(Continued)

TABLE (*Continued*) Assignment Operators (Screenshot)

S.No	Operator	Name	Example	Program	Result
10	|=	bitwise or and	a|=b	a,b=10,5 a|=b print(a)	15
11	^=	bitwise xor and	a^=b	a,b=10,5 a^=b print(a)	15
12	>>=	binary rght shift and	a>>=b	a,b=10,5 a>>=b print(a)	0
13	<<=	binary left shift and	a<<=b	a,b=10,5 a<<=b print(a)	320

Program

The preceding program is about Python program to perform assignment operations.

TABLE   Comparison Operators

S.No	Operator	Name	Syntax	Program	Result
1	==	equal to	a==b	a,b=10,5 print(a==b)	False
2	!=	not equal to	a!=b	a,b=10,5 print(a!=b)	True
3	<	less than	a<b	a,b=10,5 print(a<b)	False
4	<=	less than equal to	a<=b	a,b=10,5 print(a<=b)	False
5	>	greater than	a>b	a,b=10,5 print(a>b)	True
6	>=	greater than equal to	a>=b	a,b=10,5 print(a>=b)	True

Program

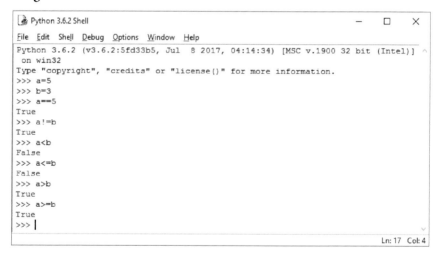

The preceding program is about Python program to perform relational operations.

TABLE   Logical Operators

S.No	Operator	Name	Example	Program	Result
1	and	logical and	a and b	a,b=10,5 print(a and b)	5
2	or	logical or	a or b	a,b=10,5 print(a or b)	10
3	not	logical not	not a	a print(not a)	False

Program

```
Python 3.6.2 Shell                                          —    □    ×
File  Edit  Shell  Debug  Options  Window  Help
Python 3.6.2 (v3.6.2:5fd33b5, Jul  8 2017, 04:14:34) [MSC v.1900 32 bit (Intel)]
on win32
Type "copyright", "credits" or "license()" for more information.
>>> a=10
>>> b=5
>>> print((a>b)and(a!=b))
True
>>> print((a<b)and(a!=b))
False
>>> print((a<b)or(a!=b))
True
>>> print(not((a<b)or(a!=b)))
False
>>>
                                                            Ln: 13  Col: 4
```

The preceding program is about Python program to perform logical operations.

TABLE   Identity Operators

S.No	Operator	Example	Program	Result
1	is	a is b	a,b=10,5 print(a is b)	False
2	is not	a is not b	a,b=10,5 print(a is not b)	True

TABLE   Membership Operators

S.No	Operator	Example	Program	Result
1	in	10 in list	l=[10,20] print(10 in l)	True
2	not in	10 not in list	print(10 not in l)	False

TABLE   Bitwise Operators

S. No	Operator	Name	Example	Program	Result
1	&	bitwise and	a&b	a,b=10,5 print(a&b)	0
2	|	bitwise or	a|b	a,b=10,5 print(a|b)	15

(*Continued*)

TABLE   (*Continued*) Bitwise Operators

S. No	Operator	Name	Example	Program	Result
3	~	bitwise not	ã	`a,b=10,5` `print(~b)`	-6
4	^	bitwise xor	a^b	`a,b=10,5` `print(a^b)`	15
5	>>	bitwise right shift	a>>b	`a,b=10,5` `print(a"b)`	0
6	<<	bitwise left shift	a<<b	`a,b=10,5` `print(a<<b)`	320

Program

```
Python 3.6.2 Shell                                          —    □    ✕
File  Edit  Shell  Debug  Options  Window  Help
Python 3.6.2 (v3.6.2:5fd33b5, Jul  8 2017, 04:14:34) [MSC v.1900 32 bit (Intel)]
on win32
Type "copyright", "credits" or "license()" for more information.
>>> a=8
>>> b=3
>>> print(a&b)
0
>>> print(a|b)
11
>>> print(~a)
-9
>>> print(~b)
-4
>>> print(a^b)
11
>>> print(a>>3)
1
>>> print(a<<3)
64
>>> print(a>>b)
1
>>> |
                                                        Ln: 21  Col: 4
```

The preceding program is about Python program to perform bitwise operations.

2.3 STRING OPERATORS

The string operators in Python are + (concatenation) and * (replication). Concatenation operator concatenates more than one string into one. The concatenation operator is not commutative, for example, ab is not equal to ba. When * sign is applied to string and a number, it replicates the string the same number of times specified by the number.

Syntax of replication operator:

- String*number
- Number*string

Program: Concatenation operator

```
s="test"
s1="ing"
print(s+s1)
```

Output

```
testing
```

Program: Replication operator

```
print("test"*3)
print(3*"sample")
print (3*"1")#outputs 111 but not 3
```

Output

```
testtesttest
samplesamplesample
111
```

2.4 OPERATOR PRECEDENCE

When more than one operator is there in the expression, to compute the expression operator precedence determines which operation to perform first. Operator associativity evaluates the operators in particular order when the operators have the same precedence.

TABLE Operator Priority

Priority	Operator	Description
1	+ -	Unary
2	**	Binary
3	/ // % *	Binary
4	+ -	Binary
5	<<= >>=	Binary
6	==!=	Binary

TABLE   Operator Precedence and Associativity

Operator Precedence Order	Meaning	Associativity
()	Parentheses	left-to-right
**	Exponent	right-to-left
+,-,~	Unary addition, Unary subtraction, and unary bitwise not	left-to-right
*, /, //, %	Multiplication, division, floor division, modulus	left-to-right
+, -	Addition, subtraction	left-to-right
<<, >> ?	Bitwise shift operators	left-to-right
&	Bitwise and	left-to-right
^	Bitwise xor	left-to-right
|	Bitwise or	left-to-right
==, !=, >, >=, <, <=, is, is not, in, not in	Comparison, identity, and membership operators	left-to-right
and, or	Logical and, logical or	left-to-right
not	Logical not	right-to-left
=, +=, -=, *=, /=, %=, &=, ^=, |=, >>=, <<=	Assignment operators	right-to-left

2.5 EXPRESSION EVALUATION

An expression is a combination of operands and operators. In Python, eval () evaluates the expression dynamically.

Syntax:

```
eval(expression[,globals[,locals]])
E.g.: eval("123+123")
246
E.g.: eval("sum[10,10,10])",{})
30
E.g.: x=100,y=100
eval("x+y")
200
In the given example both x and y are global
variables.
E.g.: eval("x+50",{},{"x":50})
100
```

In the cited example x is the local variable because it is defined inside the eval function.

2.6 INPUT () FUNCTION

The input () function can read the data entered by the programmer. The input () prompts the programmer to input some data from the console (default from keyboard). When the input () function is invoked without arguments, the function will switch the console to the input mode. The cursor blinks, and the programmer can input some keys. By pressing the enter key, the inputted data will be sent to the source code through the input functions result. The programmers must catch what the input function returns otherwise the entered data will be lost.

 Note: The default return type of the input () function is the string.

 Note: The input () function is invoked with one argument.

```
E.g.: i=input ()
```

Program

```
print("enter 2 integers")
a=int(input())
b=int(input())
print(a+b)
```

Output

```
enter 2 integers
10
30
40
```

The preceding program uses the input () function without arguments.

Program

```
a=int(input("enter integer:"))
b=int(input("enter integer:"))
c=a+b
print("sum=",c)
```

Output

```
enter integer:1
enter integer:3
sum= 4
```

The preceding program uses the input () function with arguments.

Program

```
a=input()
print(a+3)
```

Output

```
5
--------------------------------------------------------------
TypeError                   Traceback (most recent call last)
<ipython-input-22-3ae605921ae5> in <module>()
1 a=input()
----> 2 print(a+3)
TypeError: can only concatenate str (not "int") to str
```

In the preceding program it's a type error because the input returns string data type. Python does not concatenate the string and the integer. So the previous program throws the type error.

Program

```
a=input()
print(type(a))
```

Output

```
4
<class 'str'>
```

In the preceding program, the entered value is 10. Though the value 10 is an integer, the default return type value of the input () function is the string, so the output of the print function is the str (string).

Program

```
a=float(input("enter float value"))
b=float(input("enter float value"))
c=a+b
print("sum of floats=",c)
```

Output

```
enter float value1.5
enter float value3.8
sum of floats= 5.3
```

The preceding program performed sum of two floats. To convert the input value to float, there is a need to typecast the input () function with float.

Program

```
n=int(input("enter integer"))
print(n*"1")
```

Output

```
enter integer4
1111
```

The program is about replication operation by reading data from the user.

Program

```
#Ascii value
x=input("enter character:")
print("Ascii of ",x,"is",ord(x))
```

Output

```
enter character:a
Ascii of a is 97
```

The preceding program prints ascii value.

Program

```
print("%5.3e"% (123.456789))
print("%10.3e"% (123.456789))
print("%15.3e"% (123.456789))
print("%-15.3e"% (123.456789))
print("%5.3F"% (123.456789))
```

```
print("%o"% (15))
print("%5.3o"% (15))
print("%x"% (15))
print("%X"% (15))
print("%10x"% (15))
print("%10.3x"% (15))
print("%x%%"% (15))
print("%d"% (123456789))
print("%d,"% (123456789))
print("{0:4,d}".format(123456789))
print("{0:06d}".format(123))
print("{0:4,.5f}".format(123456789.123456789))
```

Output:

```
1.235e+02
1.235e+02
1.235e+02
1.235e+02
1.235E+02
17
017
f
F
f
00f
f%
123456789
123456789,
123,456,789
000123
123,456,789.12346
```

The preceding program is about formatting the numbers.

Program

```
print("this book costs {0:f} only".format(150.99))
print("this book costs {0:8f} only".format(150.99))
print("this book costs {0:.2f} only".format(150.99))
print("this book costs {0:.3f} only".format(150.99))
print("this book costs {0:.0f} only".format(150.99))
print("this book costs {0:e} only".format(150.99))
```

```
print("this book costs {0:1} only".format(150.99))
print("this book costs {0:d} only".format(150))
print("this book costs {0:8d} only".format(150))
print("this book costs {0:o} only".format(150))#octal
print("this book costs {0:b} only".format(150))#binary
print("{:d}".format(-15))
print("{:=7d}".format(-15))
print("{:=7d}".format(15))
```

Output

```
this book costs 150.990000 only
this book costs 150.990000 only
this book costs 150.99 only
this book costs 150.990 only
this book costs 151 only
this book costs 1.509900e+02 only
this book costs 150.99 only
this book costs 150 only
this book costs     150 only
this book costs 226 only
this book costs 10010110 only
- 15
- 15
15
```

The preceding program is about formatting the numbers.

2.7 LIBRARIES

2.7.1 Math and CMath Libraries

Math is the basic math module that deals with mathematical operations like sum, mean, exponential, etc., and this library is not useful with complex mathematical operations like matrix multiplication. The disadvantage is the mathematical operations performed with the math library are very slow. For instance, if we consider the example shown here, we performed the basic mathematical operations. The statement math.exp is used to find the exponent of the number. For example, *math.exp (5)* means e to the power of 5, that is, e^5. The value of e is approximately 2.17. The statement math.pi returns the value approximately 3.14. The constant *math.e* returns the value 2.17. The ceil returns the ceiling value not greater than that number. The floor returns the floor value of the given number. The *math.trunc* method returns the truncated part of the number.

TABLE   Math Functions

Function	Description
min (x1, x2 . . .)	The smallest of all its arguments
max (x1, x2 . . .)	The largest of all its arguments
pow (x, y)	The value of x**y, i.e. (2**3 = 8) (2³=8)
round (x [, n])	X rounded to n digits from the decimal point
sqrt(x)	The square root of x
abs(x)	The absolute value of x
ceil(x)	The smallest integer not less than x
floor(x)	The largest integer not greater than x
exp(x)	The exponent of x (eˣ)
log(x)	The natural logarithm of x
Iog10(x)	The base 10 logarithm of x
fabs((x)	The absolute value of x

Program

```
import math
x,y,z=10,20,30
print("min=",min(x,y,z))
print("max=",max(x,y,z))
print("sqrt of ",x,"=",math.sqrt(x))
print("round=",round(0.5))
print("power=",pow(2,3))
f=1.5
print("ceil=",math.ceil(f))
print("floor=",math.floor(f))
x=2
print("exponent=",math.exp(x))
print("log=",math.log(x))
print("log10=",math.log10(x))
x=-1
print("absolute=",abs(x))
print("absolute=",math.fabs(x))
```

Output

```
min= 10
max= 30
```

```
sqrt of 10 = 3.1622776601683795
round= 0
power= 8
ceil= 2
floor= 1
exponent= 7.38905609893065
log= 0.6931471805599453
log10= 0.3010299956639812
absolute= 1
absolute= 1.0
```

The preceding example uses some math operations and produces the output based on the mathematical operation used.

```
import math
print("exp(5)",math.exp(5))
print("Pi",math.pi)
print("Exponent",math.e)
print("factorial(5)",math.factorial(5))
print("ceil(-5)",math.ceil(-5))
print("ceil(5)",math.ceil(5))
print("ceil(5.8)",math.ceil(5.8))
print("floor(-5)",math.floor(-5))
print("floor(5)",math.floor(5))
print("floor(5.8)",math.floor(5.8))
print("trunc(-5.43)",math.trunc(-5.43))
print("pow(3,4)",math.pow(3,4))
print("pow(3,4.5)",math. pow(3,4.5))
print("pow(math.pi,4)",math. pow(math.pi,4))
print("log(4)",math.log(4))
print("log(3,4)",math.log(3,4))
print("log(math.pi,4)",math.log(math.pi,4))
print("sqrt(8)",math.sqrt(8))
```

Similarly the mathematical operations for complex numbers can be obtained by the CMath module in Python. The methods in CMath always returns a complex number. If the return value can be expressed as a real number, then the return value for the imaginary is zero. The command lines perform the mathematical operations on the complex numbers.

```
import cmath
print("cmath.pi",cmath.pi)
```

```
print("cmath.e",cmath.e)
print("sqrt(4+j5)",cmath.sqrt(4+5j))
print("cos(4+5j)",cmath.cos(4+5j))
print("sin(4+5j)",cmath.sin(4+5j))
print("tan(4+5j)",cmath.tan(4+5j))
print("asin(4+5j)",cmath.asin(4+5j))
print("acos(4+5j)",cmath.acos(4+5j))
print("atan(4+5j)",cmath.atan(4+5j))
print("sinh(4+5j)",cmath.sinh(4+5j))
print("cosh(4+5j)",cmath.cosh(4+5j))
print("tanh(4+5j)",cmath.tanh(4+5j))
print("rect(3,4)",cmath.rect(3,4))
print("log(1+2j)",cmath.log(1+2j))
print("exp(1+2j)",cmath.exp(1+2j))
```

2.7.2 SciPy Library

SciPy Python library performs mathematical operations mathematical optimization, linear algebra, etc. SciPy stands for Scientific Python. It is the scientific computation library that depends on the NumPy, which provides user-friendly and efficient-for-optimization and numerical integration. The command lines to perform SciPy library are as follows:

```
from scipy.stats import describe
import numpy as np
x=np.random.normal(size=50)
r=describe(x)
print(r)
```

Solved Examples

Program

```
a = 5
a = 1, 2, 3
print(a)
```

Output

```
(1, 2, 3)
```

Program

```
i=10
print(i!=i>5)
```

Output

```
False
```

Program

```
x=int(input("enter number:"))
y=int(input("enter number:"))
global x,y
test={"add":x+y,"sub":x-y,"mul":x*y,"div":x/y}
op=input("enter operation:")
print(test.get(op,"wrong option"))
```

Output

```
enter number:1
enter number:3
enter operation:add
4
```

EXERCISE

1. Check the result for this Python program:

   print (3**2)

   print (3. **2)

   print (3**2.)

   print (3. **2.)

2. Check the result for this Python program:

   print (3*2)

   print (3. *2)

   print (3*2.)

   print (3. *2.)

3. Check the result for this Python program:

print (8/2)

print (8. /2)

print (8/2.)

print (8. /2.)

4. Check the result for this Python program:

print (8//2)

print (8. //2)

print (8//2.)

print (8. //2.)

5. Check the result for this Python program:

print (-8//2)

print (8. //-2)

print (-8//2.)

print (-8. //2.)

6. Check the result for this Python program:

print (8%2)

print (8.5%2)

print (8%2.5)

print (8.5%2.5)

7. Run this Python program and check the result:

print (8 + 2)

print (-8.5 + 2)

print (-8 + 2.5)

print (8. +2.5)

8. Run this Python program and check the result:

   print (8–2)

   print (-8.5–2)

   print (-8–2.5)

   print (8.-2.5)

9. What is the output of the following Python program?

   print ((4**2) +5%2–3*8)

10. What is the output of the following Python program?

    print ((4%2),5**2, (5 + 4**3))

11. Write a Python program, create two variables, and assign different values to them. Perform various arithmetic operations on them. Try to print a string and an integer together on one line, for example, "sum=" and total (sum of all variables).

12. Check the output for the following line:

    print (5==5)

13. Check the output for the following line:

    print (5==5.)

14. Run this Python program and check the result:

    x,y,z=5,6,7

    print(x>y)

    print(x>z)

15. Run this Python program and check the result:

    x,y,z=1,2,3

    print(x>y)

    print((z-2) ==x)

16. Run this Python program and check the result:

```
x=5
y=5.0
z="5"
if(x==y):
print(x)
if (x==int(z)):
print(x)
```

## CHAPTER 3

Decision-Making and Conditionals

3.1 INTRODUCTION

Conditional statements can check the conditions and accordingly change the behavior of the program.

Python programming language supports different decision-making statements:

- If statement
- If-else statement
- Nested if statement
- elif statement

Python language considers non-zero, non-null values as TRUE and zero, null values as FALSE.

3.2 IF STATEMENT

The condition after the if statement is the Boolean expression. If the condition becomes true, then the specified block of statement runs, otherwise nothing happens.

Syntax

```
if condition:
#Execute the indented block if true
Statement-1
Statement-2
Statement-3
Statement-4
```

Necessary elements for the if statement:

1. The if keyword.

2. One or more white spaces.

3. An expression whose value is intercepted as true or false. If the expression is interpreted as true, then the indented block will be executed. If the expression that is evaluated is false, the indented block will be omitted, and the next instruction after the indented block level will be executed.

4. A colon followed by a newline.

5. An indented set of statements.

Program

```
a,b=10,5
if(a<b):
      print(" a is smaller than b")
if(b<a):
      print(" b is smaller than a")
```

Output

```
b is smaller than a
```

In the preceding program, the first if condition becomes false, so the corresponding print statement was not executed, and the second if statement became true, so the corresponding print statement gets executed.

3.3 IF-ELSE STATEMENT

If the condition evaluates to true, then the if block will be executed otherwise the else block will be executed.

Syntax

```
if condition:
#Execute the indented block if true
Statement-1
Statement-2
else:
#Execute the indented block if condition meets false
Statement-3
Statement-4
```

Note: Two else statements after an if statement throws error.

Program

```
# python program to find the maximum of two numbers
def maximum(a, b):
    if a >= b:
        return a
    else:
        return b
# main code
a = 2
b = 4
print(maximum(a, b))
```

Output

```
4
```

The preceding program finds max of two numbers using decision-making statements.

Program

```
#Find maximum of two numbers using ternary operator
num1 = int(input("Enter the num1: "))
```

```
num2 = int(input("Enter the num2: "))
# printing the maximum value
print("The maximum of all values is",(num1 if num1 >= num2
else num2))
Enter the num1: 3
Enter the num2: 5
The maximum of all values is 5
```

The preceding program finds max of two numbers by using the ternary operator.

3.4 NESTED-IF-ELSE STATEMENT

Nested-if-else has different forms.

Syntax-1

```
if condition1:
#Execute the indented block if true
if condition2:
Statement-1
Statement-2
else:
#Execute the indented block if condition mets false
if condition3:
Statement-3
Statement-4
```

Syntax-2

```
if condition1:
#Execute the indented block if true
if condition2:
Statement-1
Statement-2
else:
Statement-3
Statement-4
else:
#Execute the indented block if condition mets false
if condition3:
Statement-4
Statement-5
```

Synatx-3

```
if condition1:
#Execute the indented block if true
if condition2:
Statement-1
Statement-2
else:
Statement-3
Statement-4
else:
#Execute the indented block if condition mets false
if condition3:
Statement-5
Statement-6
else:
Statement-7
Statement-8
```

Syntax-4

```
if condition1:
#Execute the indented block if true
if condition2:
Statement-1
Statement-2
if condition3:
Statement-3
Statement-4
```

Syntax-5

```
if condition1:
#Execute the indented block if condition 1 is true
if condition2:
Statement-1
Statement-2
if condition3:
Statement-3
Statement-4
else:
#Execute the indented block if condition 3 is false
Statement-5
Statement-6
```

Syntax-6

```
if condition1:
#Execute the indented block if true
if condition2:
Statement-1
Statement-2
if condition3:
Statement-3
Statement-4
else:
#Execute the indented block if condition 1 is false
Statement-5
Statement-6
```

Program

```
year = 2000
if (year % 4) == 0:
      if (year % 100) == 0:
            if (year % 400) == 0:
                 print("{0} is a leap year".
format(year))
            else:
                 print("{0} is not a leap year".
format(year))
            else:
            print("{0} is a leap year".format(year))
else:
      print("{0} is not a leap year".format(year))
```

Output

```
2000 is a leap year
```

The preceding program checks whether a year is a leap year or not.

3.5 ELIF STATEMENT

Syntax

```
If condition 1:
Statements-1
elif condition 2:
```

```
#Execute the indented block if the condition-1 becomes
false
Statements-2
elif condition 3:
#Execute the indented block if all the above two
conditions become false
. . .. . . . . . .
elif condition-n:
#Execute the indented block if all the above n-1
conditions become false
Statements-n
else:
#Execute the indented block if all the above
conditions become false
statement
```

In the elif statement, else is always the last branch, and the else block is an optional block.

Program

```
#Calculating Grade
m1=int(input("enter m1:"))
m2=int(input("enter m2:"))
m3=int(input("enter m3:"))
p=(int)(m1+m2+m3/3)
if(p>90):
print("Grade-A")
elif (p>80 and p<=90):
print("Grade-B")
elif (p>60 and p<=80):
print("Grade-c")
elif (p>60 and p<=45):
print("Pass")
else:
print("Fail")
```

Output

```
enter m1:78
enter m2:89
enter m3:94
Grade-A
```

The preceding program calculates grade using elif.

3.6 WHILE

While loop repeats the execution if the condition evaluates to true. If the condition is false for the first time, the while loop body is not executed even once. The loop body should be able to change the condition value because if the condition is true at the beginning, the loop body may run continuously to infinity.

Syntax

```
while condition:
# Indent block is executed if the condition evaluates
to true
statement 1
statement 2
statement 3
statement 4
```

Program

```
# Python3 program to find Smallest of
#three integers withoutcomparison operators
def smallest(x, y, z):
c = 0
while (x and y and z) :
x = x-1
y = y-1
z = z-1
c = c + 1
return c
# Driver Code
x = 12
y = 15
z = 5
print("Minimum of 3 numbers is",
smallest(x, y, z))
```

Output

```
Mininum of 3 numbers is 5
```

The preceding program finds min of three numbers using while loop.

Program

```
#program to Display the Multiplication Table
num = int(input(" Enter the number : "))
i = 1
# using for loop to iterate multiplication 10 times
print("Multiplication Table of : ")
while i<=10:
        num = num * 1
        print(num,'×',i,'=',num*i)
        i += 1
```

Output

```
Enter the number : 5
Multiplication Table of :
5 × 1 = 5
5 × 2 = 10
5 × 3 = 15
5 × 4 = 20
5 × 5 = 25
5 × 6 = 30
5 × 7 = 35
5 × 8 = 40
5 × 9 = 45
5 × 10 = 50
```

The preceding program prints the multiplication table using while loop.

3.7 FOR LOOP

The for loop is used to iterate a sequence range of the items of different data structures like list, tuple, string, etc.

Syntax

```
for value in sequence-range:
        loop body
```

Explanation about the for syntax is discussed in the next section:

- For keyword.

- The variable after the for keyword is the control variable of the loop, automatically counts the loop turns.

- The in keyword.

- The range () function. The range () function accepts only the integers as its arguments, and it generates the sequence of integers.

Body of the for loop. Sometimes the pass keyword inside the loop body is nothing but the empty loop body. The body of the loop may consist of the if statement, if-else statement, elif statement, while loop.

Note: The range () function may accept the three arguments: start, end, increment. The default value of the increment is 1.

Program

```
#range with one argument
for seq in range(10):
        print(seq)
0
1
2
3
4
5
6
7
8
9
```

The preceding program uses for ... range with one argument to print a sequence of numbers from 0 to 9.

Program

```
#range with two argument
for seq in range(5,10):
        print(seq)
```

Output

```
5
6
7
8
9
```

The preceding program uses for . . . range with two arguments to print a sequence of numbers from 5 to 10 with step value 1.

Program

```
#range with three argument and argument is ascending
for seq in range(50,1000,100):
      Print(seq)
```

Output

```
50
150
250
350
450
550
650
750
850
950
```

The preceding program uses for . . . range with three arguments, and argument is ascending to print a sequence of numbers from 50 to 1000 with step value of 100.

Program

```
#range with three argument and argument is descending
for seq in range(100,10,-10):
      print(seq)
100
90
80
70
```

```
60
50
40
30
20
```

The preceding program uses for . . . range with three arguments, and argument is descending to print a sequence of numbers from 100 to 10 with step value of – 10.

Program:

```
#Negative range()
for i in range(-1, -11, -1):
        print(i, end=', ')
```

Output:

```
-1, -2, -3, -4, -5, -6, -7, -8, -9, -10
```

The previous program uses the negative values for start, end, and the step values.

3.8 NESTED FOR LOOPS

The nested for loop is used to iterate different data structures and iterable data objects.

In Python, a for loop inside another for loop.

Syntax

```
# outer for loop
for element in sequence
        # inner for loop
        for element in sequence:
                body of inner for loop
        body of outer for loop
```

Output:

```
1 2 3 4 5 6 7 8 9
2 4 6 8 10 12 14 16 18
3 6 9 12 15 18 21 24 27
4 8 12 16 20 24 28 32 36
```

Program

```
n=int(input("enter number:"))
for i in range(1,n+1):
        for j in range(1,i+1):
                print(i,end=" ")
        print()
```

Output

```
enter number:5
1
2 2
3 3 3
4 4 4 4
5 5 5 5 5
```

The preceding program prints the numbers in a specific pattern.

Program

```
n=int(input("enter number:"))
for i in range(1,n+1):
        for j in range(1,i+1):
                print(j,end=" ")
        print()
```

Output

```
enter number:5
1
1 2
1 2 3
1 2 3 4
1 2 3 4 5
```

The preceding program prints the numbers in a specific pattern.

3.9 NESTED WHILE

A while loop inside another while loop.

Syntax

```
while expression:
        while expression:
                statement(s)
        statement(s)
```

Program

```
#Strong number
n=int(input("enter number"))
t=n
sum=0
while(n!,=0):
i,f=1,1
r=n%10
while{i<=r):
f*=i
i+=1
sum+=f
n//=10
if(t==sum):
print(t,"is strong number")
else:
print(t,"is not strong number")
```

Output

```
enter number9
9 is not strong number
```

The preceding program checks whether the given number is a strong number or not using the nested while.

Program

```
# multiplication table using nested while
n=2
while 1:
i=1;
```

```
while i<=10:
print("%d x %d = %d\n"%(n,i,n*i));
i = i+1;
choice = int(input("Do you want to continue printing
the table, press 0 for no?"))
if choice == 0:
break;
n=n+1
```

Output

```
2 x 1 = 2
2 x 2 = 4
2 x 3 = 6
2 x 4 = 8
2 x 5 = 10
2 x 6 = 12
2 x 7 = 14
2 x 8 = 16
2 x 9 = 18
2 x 10 = 20
Do you want to continue printing the table, press 0
for no?0
```

The preceding program prints the multiplication table using the nested while.

3.10 USING ELSE STATEMENT WITH FOR LOOP

If the for loop contains any of the break statement, then the else statement will not be executed.

Syntax

```
for statement
# For loop code
else:
# Else block code
```

Program

```
for i in range(1, 5):
      print(i)
else: # Executed because no break in for
      print("No Break")
```

Output

```
1
2
3
4
No Break
```

3.11 THE PASS STATEMENT IN FOR LOOP

If we want to implement the code in the future and now, it should not be empty. If we empty for loop, then the interpreter throws an error. To prevent such type of error, pass will be used. The pass statement constructs the body of the for loop that does nothing.

Syntax

```
for val in sequence:
     pass
```

Program

```
for i in "this is to test":
     if i=="e" or i=="o":
           pass
     else:
           print(i,end=" ")
```

Output

```
this is t tst
```

The preceding program uses the pass statement in for loop.

3.12 BREAK STATEMENT

Break – exists the loop immediately and unconditionally ends the loop; the control goes to the next instruction after the loop body.

Syntax

```
break
```

Program

```
# Use of break statement inside the loop
for val in "string":
        if val == "i":
                break
        print(val)
```

Output

```
s
t
r
```

The preceding program uses the break statement in the for loop. The for loop iterates through the string literal "string" and when the character "i" is encountered the for loop breaks.

Program

```
n = 1
while n < 5:
        n += 1
        if n == 3:
                break
        print(n)
```

Output

```
2
```

The preceding program is about break statement in while loop.

Program

```
for i in range(3):
for j in range(2):
if j == i:
break
print(i, j)
```

Output

```
1 0
2 0
2 1
```

The preceding program is about break loop in nested for loops.

Program

```
#break inner loop while
while True:
print ("In outer loop")
i = 0
while True:
print ("In inner loop")
if i >= 5: break
i += 1
print("Got out of inner loop, still inside outer
loop")
break
```

Output

```
In outer loop
In inner loop
In inner loop
In inner loop
In inner loop
In inner loop
In inner loop
Got out of inner loop, still inside outer loop
```

The preceding program uses the break statement in nested inner while loop.

3.13 CONTINUE

Continue – skips the remaining body of the loop.

Syntax

```
continue
```

Program

```
# Program to show the use of continue statement inside
loops
for val in "string":
        if val == "i":
                continue
        print(val)
```

Output

```
s
t
r
n
g
```

The preceding program uses the continue statement in for loop.

Program

```
i = 1
while i <= 5:
        i = i+1
        if(i==3):
                continue
        print(i)
```

Output

```
2
4
5
6
```

The preceding program is about continue statement in while loop.

Program

```
first = [1,2,3]
second = [4,5]
for i in first:
        for j in second:
                if i == j:
```

```
                        continue
               print(i, '*', j, '=', i * j)
```

Output

```
1 * 4 = 4
1 * 5 = 5
2 * 4 = 8
2 * 5 = 10
3 * 4 = 12
3 * 5 = 15
```

The preceding program is about continue loop in nested for loops.

Program

```
i=1
while i<=2 :
        print(i,"outer ")
        j=1
        while j<=2:
                print(j,"Inner ")
                j+=1
                if(j==2):
                        continue
        i+=1;
```

Output

```
1 Outer
1 Inner
2 Inner
2 Outer
1 Inner
2 Inner
```

The preceding program is about continue statement in nested while loops.

3.14 WHILE LOOP AND THE ELSE BRANCH

The loops while and the for loop has an interesting feature in Python. The else block is executed once regardless of whether the loop has entered its loop body or not, but the else block of the while executes once.

Syntax

```
while condition:
statements
else:
statements
```

If the condition becomes false at the very first iteration, then the while loop body never executes.

Note: The else block executes after the loop finishes its execution if it has not been terminated by the break statement.

Solved examples

Program

```
for i in "test":
        if i == "s":
                break
        print(i)
```

Output

```
t
e
```

Program: The continue statement

```
for i in "test":
        if i == "s":
                continue
        print(i)
```

Output

```
t
e
t
```

Program

```
#Amstrong number
n=int(input("enter number"))
sum=0
t=n
C=0
while t>0:
c = c+1
t=t//10
t=n
while t>0:
r=t%10
sum+=(r**c)
t//=10
if n==sum:
print(n,"is amstrong number")
else:
print(n,"is not amstrong number")
```

Output

```
enter number5
5 is amstrong number
```

The preceding program checks whether the given number is amstrong number or not.

Program

```
#Factorial of a number
n=int(input("enter number"))
f=1
for i in range(1,n+1):
        f*=i
print("factorial is",f)
```

Output

```
enter number5
factorial is 120
```

The preceding program prints the factorial of the given number.

Program

```
#Reverse the number
n=int(input("enter number"))
rev=0
while(n>0):
     r=n%10
     rev=rev*10+r
     n=n//10
print("reverse number",rev)
```

Output

```
enter number123
reverse number 321
```

The preceding program prints the given number in the reverse order.

Program

```
#Palindrome Number
n=int(input("enter number"))
rev=0
t=n
while(n>0):
r=n%10
rev=rev*10+r
n=n//10
if(t==rev):
print(t," is plindrome")
else:
print(t," is not plindrome")
```

Output

```
enter number121
121 is plindrome
```

The preceding program checks whether the given number is a palindrome number or not.

Program

```
#Printing first max and the second max number
```

```
n=int(input("enter range"))
fbig,sbig=0,0
for i in range(0,n,1):
num=int(input("enter number"))
if(num>fbig:
sbig=fbig
fbig=num
if(num>sbig and num<fbig):
sbig=num
print("first max:",fbig)
print("second max:",sbig)
```

Output

```
enter range5
enter number4
enter number9
enter nubmer23
enter number45
enter number89
first max: 89
second max: 45
```

The preceding program prints first max and the second max number without using array.

Program

```
#perfect number
n=int(input("enter number"))
sum=0
for i in range(1,n):
if(n%i==0):
sum+=i
if(n==sum):
print(n,"is perfect number")
else:
print(n,"is not perfect number")
```

Output

```
enter number5
5 is not perfect number
```

The preceding program checks whether the given number is perfect or not.

Program

```
n=int(input("enter number:"))
for i in range(n,0,-1):
        for j in range(1,i+1):
                print(j,end=" ")
        print()
```

Output

```
enter number:5
1 2 3 4 5
1 2 3 4
1 2 3
1 2
1
```

The preceding program prints patterns using nested for.

Program

```
n=int(input("enter number:"))
for i in range(n,0,-1):
        for j in range(i,0,-1):
                print(j,end=" ")
        print()
```

Output

```
enter number:5
5 4 3 2 1
4 3 2 1
3 2 1
2 1
1
```

The preceding program prints patterns using nested for.

Program

```
# Python program to find the
```

```
# minimum of two numbers
def minimum(a, b):
if a <= b:
return a
else:
return b
# Driver code
a = 2
b = 4
print(minimum(a, b))
```

Output

```
2
```

The preceding program is to find in of two numbers without using min () function.

Program

```
# function computes the gross salary from basic
salary.
def calculate_gross_salary(basic_salary):
hra = 0;
da = 0;
# salary is less than 2500, hra and da is calculated
if (basic_salary < 2500):
hra = (basic_salary * 10) / 100;
da = (basic_salary * 90) / 100;
else:
hra = 1000;
da = (basic_salary * 95) / 100;
return (basic_salary + hra + da);
if __ name__ == "__main__":
# Type casting from input string into float value.
basic_salary = float(input("Enter basic salary: "));
gross_salary = calculate_gross_salary(basic_salary);
print("Gross Salary is: %f" % gross_salary);
```

Output

```
Enter basic salary: 10000
Gross Salary is: 20500.000000
```

The preceding program is for net income calculation.

Program

```
#max of 3 numbers using while loop
numbers = [1,2,5,8,4,99,3]
x = 0
lar = numbers[x]
while x < len(numbers):
if numbers[x] > lar:
lar = numbers[x]
x = x+1
print(lar)
```

Output

```
99
```

The preceding program prints the max of seven numbers using while loop.

Program

```
#Infinite loop using while
while True:
    num = int(input("Enter an integer: "))
    print("The double of",num,"is",2 * num)
```

Output

```
Enter an integer: 5
The double of 5 is 10
Enter an integer: 7
The double of 7 is 14
Enter an integer: 0
The double of 0 is 0
Enter an integer: -1
The double of -1 is -2
Enter an integer: -0.5
--------------------------------------------------------------------
ValueError              Traceback (most recent call last)
<ipython-input-132-d7b1308085a4> in <module>()
1 #1: Infinite loop using while
```

The preceding program is for the infinite loop using the while statement.

Program

```
#Program to Display the Multiplication Table
num = int(input(" Enter the number : "))
# using for loop to iterate multiplication 10 times
print("Multiplication Table of : ")
for i in range(1,11):
     print(num,'x',i,'=',num*i)
```

Output

```
Enter the number : 1
Multiplication Table of :
1 x 1 = 1
1 x 2 = 2
1 x 3 = 3
1 x 4 = 4
1 x 5 = 5
1 x 6 = 6
1 x 7 = 7
1 x 8 = 8
1 x 9 = 9
1 x 10 = 10
```

The preceding program prints the multiplication table for the given number using the for statement.

Program

```
# Python program to
# demonstrate continue
# statement
# loop from 1 to 10
for i in range(1, 11):
# If i is equals to 6,
# continue to next iteration
# without printing
if i == 6:
continue
else:
# otherwise print the value
```

```
# of i
print(i, end = " ")
```

Output

```
1 2 3 4 5 7 8 9 10
```

The preceding uses the continue statement to print the numbers.

Program

```
#Infinite loop using for
import itertools
for i in itertools.count():
     print(i)
```

The preceding program is the infinite loop using the or control statement.

Program

```
#Pascal triangle
n=int(input("enter range"))
for i in range(0,n):
for s in range(0,n-i):
print(end=" ")
for j in range(0,i+1):
if(j==0 or i==0):
c=1
else:
c=(int)(c*(i-j+1)/j)
print(c,end=" ")
print()
```

Output

```
enter range5
1
1 1
1 2 1
1 3 3 1
1 4 6 4 1
```

The preceding program prints the pascal triangle.

Program

```
#check even or odd using ternary operator
x=int(input("enter number"))
s="even" if x%2==0 else "odd"
print(x,"is",s)
```

Output

```
enter number5
5 is odd
```

The preceding program used the ternary operator to check whether the given number is even or odd.

Program

```
#Max of three numbers using ternary operator
x=int(input("enter number"))
y=int(input("enter number"))
z=int(input("enter number"))
max= x if x>y and x>z else y if y>z else z
print("max:",max)
```

Output

```
enter number5
enter number9
enter number11
max: 11
```

The preceding program used the ternary operator to find the max of the three numbers.

Program

```
#Max of four numbers using ternary operator
p=int(input("enter number"))
q=int(input("enter number"))
r=int(input("enter number"))
s=int(input("enter number"))
max= p if p>q and p>r and p>s else
q if q>r and q>s else r if r>s else s
print("max:",max)
```

Output

```
enter number4
enter number8
enter number3
enter number2
max: 8
```

The preceding program used the ternary operator to find the max of the four numbers.

Program

```python
# Python program to find the largest
# number among the three numbers
def maximum(a, b, c):
if (a >= b) and (a >= c):
largest = a
elif (b >= a) and (b >= c):
largest = b
else:
largest = c
return largest
# Driven code
a = 10
b = 14
c = 12
print(maximum(a, b, c))
```

Program

```python
# Python3 program to find Smallest
# of three integers using division operator to find
# minimum of three numbers
def smallest(x, y, z):
if (not (y / x)): # Same as "if (y < x)"
return y if (not (y / z)) else z
return x if (not (x / z)) else z
# Driver Code
if __name__ == "__main__":
x = 78
y = 88
z = 68
```

```
print("Minimum of 3 numbers is",
      smallest(x, y, z))
```

Output

```
Minimum of 3 numbers is 68
```

Program

```
#Even inclusive range()
step = 2
for i in range(2, 20 + step, step):
    print(i, end=' ')
```

Output

```
2 4 6 8 10 12 14 16 18 20
```

Program

```
#range() indexing and slicing
range1 = range(0, 10)
# first number (start number) in range
print(range1[0])
# access 5th number in range
print(range1[5])
#Output 5
# access last number
print(range1[range1.stop - 1])
```

Output

```
0
5
9
```

Program

```
#Negative indexing range
# negative indexing
# access last number
print(range(10)[-1])
# output 9
# access second last number
print(range(10)[-2])
```

Output

```
9
8
```

Program

```
#Slicing range
for i in range(10)[3:8]:
      print(i, end=' ')
```

Output

```
3 4 5 6 7
```

Program

```
#Reverse range
for i in reversed(range(10, 21, 2)):
      print(i, end=' ')
```

Output

```
20 18 16 14 12 10
```

Program

```
#One-Line while Loops
n = 5
while n> 0: n -= 1; print(n)
```

Output

```
4
3
2
1
0
```

Program

```
# Use of break statement inside the loop
for val in "string":
      if val == "i":
            break
      print(val)
```

Output

```
s
t
r
```

Program

```
#concatenate two or more range functions using the
itertools
from itertools import chain
a1 = range(10,0,-2)
a2 = range(30,20,-2)
a3 = range(50,40,-2)
final = chain(a1,a2,a3)
print(final)
```

Output

```
<itertools.chain object at 0x7f2e824a6ad0>
```

EXERCISE

1. Write a Python program. Use the while loop and continuously ask the programmer to enter the word unless the programmer enters the word "quit". By entering the word "quit", the loop should terminate.

2. Write a Python program to read an input from the user and separate the vowels and consonants in the entered word.

3. Write a Python program to read an input from the user and to print the uppercase of the entered word.

## CHAPTER 4

Strings

Python does not provide a character data type. String is a data type in Python language, and the programmers can create a string by surrounding characters in quotes.

4.1 STRING CREATION

Python considers single quotes the same as double quotes, and string index and negative index representation is shown in Figure 4.1.

For example:

```
s='this is to test' #single quote example
s1="this is to test" # double quote example
```

Syntax

```
String name="content inside quotes"
```

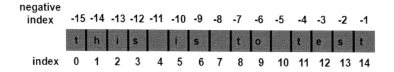

FIGURE 4.1   String index and negative index representation.

DOI: 10.1201/9781003414322-4

4.2 ACCESSING VALUES TO A STRING

To access the values of the string, use the slicing operator (:) and the indexing operator ([]).

Program

```
s="this is to test"
print(s[0])
print(s[13])
```

Output

```
t
s
```

The preceding program used the indexing operator ([]) to display the string.

Program

```
s="this is to test"
print(s[0:])
print(s[5:10])
print(s[-3])
print(s[-7:-3])
```

Output

```
this is to test
is to
e
to t
```

The preceding program used the slicing operator (:) to display the string.

Program

```
s="this is to test"
print(s)
print("s[:6]--",s[:6])
print("s[4:]--",S[4:])
print("s[-1]--",s[-1])
print("s[-2:]--",s[-2:])
print("s[-2:5]--",s[-2:5])
print("s[5:-2]--",s[5:-2])
print("s[::-1]--",s[::-1])
```

```
print("s[-14]--",s[-14])
print("s[-15]--",s[-15])
print("s[:-1]--",s[:-1])
print("s[5:-1]--",s[5:-1])
print("s[5:-2]--",s[5:-2])
print("s[-5:-2]--",s[-5:-2])
```

Output

```
this is to test
s[:6]-- this i
s[4:]-- is to test
s[-1]-- t
s[-2:]-- st
s[-2:5]--
s[5:-2]-- is to te
s[::-1]-- tset ot si siht
s[-14]-- h
s[-15]-- t
s[:-1]-- this is to tes
s[5:-1]-- is to tes
s[5:-2]-- is to te
s[-5:-2]-- te
```

In the preceding program is a string displaying using index notations.

Program

```
s="this is to test"
print(s[15])
```

Output

```
IndexError                Traceback (most recent call last)
<ipython-input-12-e2bc36c787f4> in <module>()
1 s="this is to test"
----> 2 print(s[15])
IndexError: string index out of range
```

The preceding program tries to print index out of range.

Program

```
s="this is to test"
print(s[1.5])
```

Output

```
TypeError                Traceback (most recent call last)
<ipython-input-13-8a4d10de04c8> in <module>()
1 s="this is to test"
----> 2 print(s[1.5])
TypeError: string indices must be integers
```

The preceding program gives non-integer index value to retrieve string content.

4.3 MODIFY EXISTING STRING

The programmers can alter an existing string by reassigning another string to the variable.

Program

```
s="this is to test"
print(s)
s="india"
print(s)
```

Output

```
this is to test
india
```

We can modify the part of the string by using the slicing operator.

Program

```
s="this is to test"
print(s[0:])
print ("updated string :- ", s[:6] + 'Python')
```

Output

```
this is to test
Updated String :- this iPython
```

In the preceding program, from the six character onwards, the string has been modified as the string Python. Modified the string "s to test" with the string "python".

Program

```
s="Vijayawada"
print(s)
s="pyhton"
print(s)
s="string example"
print(s)
s="this is to test"
print(s)
```

Output

```
vijayawada
pyhton
string example
this is to test
```

The preceding program updates the string.

4.4 ESCAPE CHARACTERS

An escape character becomes interpreted in a single quote as well as double quote. An escape character can be embodied with backslash notation. The subsequent table, Table 4.1, is a list of escape or non-printable characters.

TABLE 4.1   Escape Characters

Backslash Notation	Description
\a	Bell or alert
\b	Backspace
\e	Escape
\f	Form feed
\n	New line
\r	Carriage return
\s	Space
\t	Tab
\v	Vertical tab
\x	Character x
\xnn	Hexadecimal notation

Note: print ("\\") produces output \.

Program

```
print("\\")
```

Output

\

4.5 STRING SPECIAL CHARACTERS

The special characters to access the string is tabulated in Table 4.2.

TABLE 4.2   String Special Characters

Operator	Description
+	Concatenation
*	Repetition
[]	Slice
[:]	Range slice
In	Membership operator – returns true if a specified character exists in a string
not in	Membership operator – returns false if a specified character exists in a string
%	String formatting
r/r	Raw string

Program

```
s="python"
print(s+s)
print(s+s+s)
print(s*4)
print('t' in s)
print('t' not in s)
print("12345"*3)
```

Output

```
pythonpython
pythonpythonpython
pythonpythonpythonpython
True
False
123451234512345
```

The preceding program applies the concatenation, membership, and the replication operator on strings.

4.6 STRING FORMATTING OPERATOR

The % operator is unique to strings. The following table consists of collection of symbols that can be utilized with %. Different string formatting operators are tabulated in Table 4.3

TABLE 4.3   String Formatting Operators

Format operator	Description
%c	Character
%i	String conversion
%s	Signed Integer
%d	Signed Integer
%u	Unsigned integer
%o	Octal integer
%x	Hexadecimal integer – lowercase
%X	Hexadecimal integer – uppercase
%e	Exponent notation – lowercase
%E	Exponent notation – lowercase
%f	Floating point
%g	Shorter form %f and %e
%G	Shorter form %f and %E

Program

```
s="{}{}{}{}".format('this', 'is', 'for', 'test')
print(s)
s="{} {} {} {}".format('this', 'is', 'for', 'test')
print(s)
s="{3}{2}{1}{0}".format('this', 'is', 'for', 'test')
print(s)
s="{t}{i}{f}{e}".format(t='this',i='is',f='for',e='t
est')
print(s)
s="{}, string format example".format("pyhton")
print(s)
s="string example in {}".format("pyhton")
print{s)
s="this example is for {}, string".format("pyhton")
print(s)
```

Output

```
thisisfortest
this is for test
testforisthis
thisisfortest
pyhton, string format example
string example in pyhton
this example is for pyhton, string
```

The preceding program formats the string using format ().

Program

```
s="this is to test"
print(s)
s1='this is to test'
print(s1)
s2="'this is to test'"
print(s2)
s3='"this is to test"'
print(s3)
s4='''this is
to
test'''
print(s4)
s5="this is \n to test"
print(s5)
s5="this is \t to test"
print(s5)
print("'{}'".format("this is to test"))
print('"{}"'.format("this is to test"))
st="this is to test"
print("%s"%st)
print("\\%s\\"%st)
print("\"%s\""%st)
print("It\'s pyhton \'String\' testing")
print("\"Python\" String example")
print(r"\"Python\" String example")#raw string
print(R"\"Python\" String example")#raw string
print("{:.7}".format("this is to test"))
```

```
this is to test
this is to test
'this is to test'
"this is to test"
this is
to
test
this is
to test
this is      to test
'this is to test'
"this is to test"
this is to test
\this is to test\
"this is to test"
It's python 'String' testing
"Python" String example
\"Python" String example
\"Python\" String example
this is
```

The preceding program displays the string in different formats.

Program

```
print("this {0:10} is to test {1:10} {2:10}".format
('example','pyhton','string'))
print("this {0:>10} is to test {1:>10} {2:>10}".format
('example','pyhton','string'))
print("this {0:<10} is to test {1:<10} {2:<10}".format
('example','pyhton','string'))
print("this {0:^10} is to test {1:^10} {2:^10}".format
('example','pyhton','string'))
print("this {0:@>10} is to test {1:*>10}{2:&>10}".format
('example','pyhton','string'))
print("this {0:$<10} is to test {1:%<10} {2:~<10}".format
('example','pyhton','string'))
print("this {0:#^10} is to test {1:!^10} {2:*^10}".format
('example','pyhton','string'))
```

Output:

```
this example       is to test  pyhton        string
this example       is to test  pyhton        string
this example       is to test  pyhton        string
this example       is to test  pyhton        string
this @@@example    is to test  ****pyhton    &&&&string
this example$$$    is to test  pyhton%%%     string~~~~
this #example##    is to test  !!pyhton!!    **string**
```

The preceding program formats the strings using the alignments by format ().

4.7 TRIPLE QUOTES

Triple quotes permit the string to span multiple lines.

Program

```
s="""this is
to test"""
print(s)
```

Output

```
this is
to test
```

4.8 UNICODE STRINGS

In Python the normal strings are accumulated as the 8-bit ASCII, whereas the unicode strings are saved as the 16-bit values.

Note: Unicode strings apply the prefix u; raw strings use the prefix r.

Program

```
print(u'test')
```

Output

```
test
```

4.9 BUILT-IN STRING METHODS

Some of the predefined string methods to handle strings are tabulated in Table 4.4.

TABLE 4.4   Built-In String Methods

Method	Description
capitalize ()	Capitalizes first letter of string.
Count (str, beg=0, end=len(string))	Counts how many times str occurs in string or in substring of string if starting index beg and ending index end are given.
find (st, beg=0, end=len(string))	Determines if st occurs in string or in a substring of string form starting index beg and ending index end are given returns index if found and − 1 otherwise.
join (seq)	Merges the string.
len (st)	Returns the length of the string.
lower ()	Converts all uppercase letters in string to lowercase.
max (str)	Returns the max alphabetical character from the string str.
min (str)	Returns the min alphabetical character from the string str.
replace (old, new[, max])	Replaces all occurrences of old in string with new or at most max occurrences if max given.
rstrip ()	Performs both lstrip () and rstrip () on string.
swapcase ()	Inverts case for all the letters in the string.
upper ()	Converts lowercase letters in string to uppercase.
zfill (width)	Left padded with zeros to a total of width characters.

Program

```
s="Vijayawada"
print(s)
s[0]='b'
```

Output

```
Vijayawada
--------------------------------------------------------------------
TypeError              Traceback (most recent call last)
<ipython-input-18-1f023e1b5186> in <module>()
1.s="Vijayawada"
2 print(s)
---->3 s[0]='b'
TypeError: 'str' object does not support item assignment
```

The preceding program tries to modify the string using = operator. The interpreter throws error. To modify the string, we must use the predefined method replace ().

Program

```
s="Vijayawada"
print(s)
print(s.replace('V','B'))
```

Output

```
Vijayawada
Bijayawada
```

The preceding program modifies some specific portion of the string.

Program

```
s="this is to test"
print(s.capitalize())
print(s.lower())
print(s.swapcase())
print(s.title())
print(s.upper())
print(s.count('t'))
print(s.find('s'))
print(s.index('is'))
print(s.rfind('is'))
print(s.rindex('is'))
print(s.startswith('this'))
print(s.endswith('t'))
print("  this is to test  ".lstrip())
print("  this is to test  ".rstrip())
print("  this is to test  ".strip())
print(s.partition('@'))
print(s.rpartition('@'))
print(s.split())
print(s.rsplit())
print(s.splitlines())
print("this \t is \v to \b test".splitlines())
print("this is to test".casefold())
print("THIS IS TO TEST".casefold())
print(s.encode())
```

Output

```
This is to test
this is to test
THIS IS TO TEST
This Is To Test
THIS IS TO TEST
4
3
2
5
5
True
True
this is to test
this is to test
this is to test
('this is to test', '', '')
('', '', 'this is to test')
['this', 'is', 'to', 'test']
['this', 'is', 'to', 'test']
['this is to test']
['this \t is ', 'to \x08 test']
this is to test
this is to test
b'this is to test'
```

The preceding program checks some of the predefined methods for string.

4.10 DELETING STRING

The users can delete the entire string but not part of the string.

Program

```
s="python"
print("the given sting is: ",s)
del s
print(s)
```

Output

```
the given sting is:  python
----------------------------------------------------------------
```

```
NameError     Traceback (most recent call last)
<ipython-input-17-369fdc4f776a> in <module>()
2 print("the given sting is: ",s)
3 del s
----> 4 print(s)
NameError: name 's' is not defined
```

The preceding program deletes the string s. After deleting the string, when the user tries to retrieve the string, the name error, the string not defined is thrown.

Program

```
s="this is to test"
del s[1]
```

Output

```
-------------------------------------------------------------------------
TypeError     Traceback (most recent call last)
<ipython-input-8-6bfc7ff42e45> in <module>()
1 s="this is to test"
----> 2 del s[1]
TypeError: 'str' object doesn't support item deletion
```

The preceding program tries to delete the part of the string. Python does not support deleting the part of the string, so we got the error.

EXERCISE

1. Write a Python program using the new line and the escape characters to match the expected result as follows:

   "This is"

   "to test"

   "Python language"

2. Write a program to count the number of the characters in the string (Do not use the predefined method).

3. Access the first three characters and the last two characters from the given string.

4. Count the number of occurrences of the first character in the given string.

5. Access the longest word in the given sentence.

6. Exchange the first and the last characters of each word in a sentence.

7. Insert the character <> in the middle of each word in a sentence.

8. Access the words whose length is less than 3.

9. Reverse the words in a sentence.

10. Print the index of the characters of the string.

11. Replace the vowel with a specified character.

12. Remove the duplicate characters from the string.

## CHAPTER 5

Lists

5.1 INTRODUCTION

List is a collection of elements, but each element may be a different type. List is a data type in Python programming language, which can be written as a list of commas separated values between square brackets. Creating a list is putting different comma separated values between square brackets. The list is a type in python used to store multiple objects. It is an ordered and mutable collection of elements.

The value inside the bracket that selects one element of the list is called an index, while the operation of selecting an element from the list is called as indexing. List indexing is shown in Figure 5.1, and the specific indication of the index is shown in Figure 5.2.

```
L1= ['this', 'is', 'to', 'test']
```

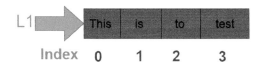

FIGURE 5.1   List indexing.

DOI: 10.1201/9781003414322-5   **91**

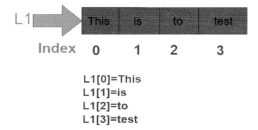

FIGURE 5.2   Specific indexing location and its content of the list.

```
L4= ["a", "b", "c", "d", "e"]
```

List indices start at 0, and lists can be sliced, concatenated, and soon.

Note: The index may be the expression or the number.

Note: + works on lists as concatenation operator and * works as repetition operator

5.2 CHARACTERISTICS OF LISTS

The important characteristics of Python lists are as follows:

Lists are ordered.

Lists can contain any arbitrary objects.

List elements can be accessed by index.

Lists can be nested to arbitrary depth.

Lists are mutable.

Lists are dynamic.

The built functions and the predefined methods are tabulated in Table 5.1 and Table 5.2.

TABLE 5.1 Built-In Functions in Lists

Function	Description
cmp(list1, Iist2)	Compares the elements of the two lists
len(list)	Calculates the length of the list
max(list)	Returns the maximum element of the list
min(list)	Returns the minimum of the list
list(sequences)	Converts any sequence to the list elements
sum ()	Summarizes all the elements in the list

TABLE 5.2 The Predefined Methods for List in Python

Method	Description
list.append(obj)	Adds an element at the end of the list
list.count(obj)	Counts the number of elements in the list
list.extend(seq)	Adds all elements of the list to another list
list.index(obj)	Returns the index of the first matched item
list.insert(index,obj)	Inserts the elements at the defined index
list.pop(obj=list [-])	Removes an element at the given index
list.remove(obj)	Removes the list
list.reverse()	Reverses the order of elements of the list
list.sort([func])	Sorts items in a list in the ascending order

5.3 DECISION-MAKING IN LISTS

Decision-making plays a vital role to access/update/delete elements in the python list. The detailed example with explanation is given in the following sections.

For loop

```
r = range(2, 20, 3)
l = list()
for x in r :
l.append(x)
print(1)
```

Result

```
[2, 5, 8, 11, 14, 17]
```

In the cited example, list () is the list constructor and l is the list object created using the list constructor. The variable r was created using the range with the starting element of 2 and the ending element with 20 and increment was 3; that is, the first element is 2, the second element is 5, the third element is 8, and so on. By using the for loop, the r variable elements are appended to the list l by using the predefined method append of the list at line number 4. At line 5 the list is displayed using the print statement.

While loop

```
l1 = [1, 3, 5, 7, 9]
l = len(l1)
i = 0
while i < l
print(l1[i])
i += 1
1
3
5
7
9
```

In the cited example, l1 is the list, which consists of five integer elements. Using the while loop to print the list l1 elements. The variable i is used as the index variable. The while condition is i<l, that is, the loop repeats for the length of the list. If the condition is true, then it prints the list element based on the index location and incrementing the index. If the while is false, then the while loop gets terminated.

5.3.1 Range

The range function generates the numbers based on the given specified values. The syntax is

```
range (Start, End, Step)
```

The start indicator is the starting element, end indicator is the end element, and step indicator is used to increment the elements.

```
print(list(range(6)))
```

Result

```
[0, 1, 2, 3, 4, 5]
```

In the cited example, start is the optional, so it is considered as the value 0 because 0 is the default start value, and the end element is number 6, and step is optional, so the default step is +1.

```
r = range(2, 20, 5)
l = list(r)
print(l)
```

Result

```
[2, 7, 12, 17]
```

In the cited example, start value is 2 and the end element is number 20 and step is 5. The first element is 2, the second element is (first element + step that is $2+5=7$) 7, the third element is (second element + step=>$7+5=12$)12 and so on.

5.4 ACCESSING VALUES IN THE LIST

To retrieve values in the list, use the square brackets for slicing along with the index or indices to acquire value presented at that index. For example:

Example: list slicing

```
L1= ['this', 'is', 'to', 'test']
print(L1[0])
print(L1[0:3])
```

Result

```
this
['this', 'is', 'to']
```

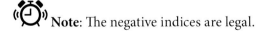 **Note:** The negative indices are legal.

An element with an index equal to – 1 is the last element in the list. The index – 2 is the one before last element in the list. The negative index for the list is shown in Figure 5.3, and the list that contains different data types along with index and negative index is shown in Figure 5.4.

```
L1= ['this', 'is', 'to', 'test']
```

FIGURE 5.3 Negative index.

```
L3= [1.1,2.2,3.3,4.4, "test"]
```

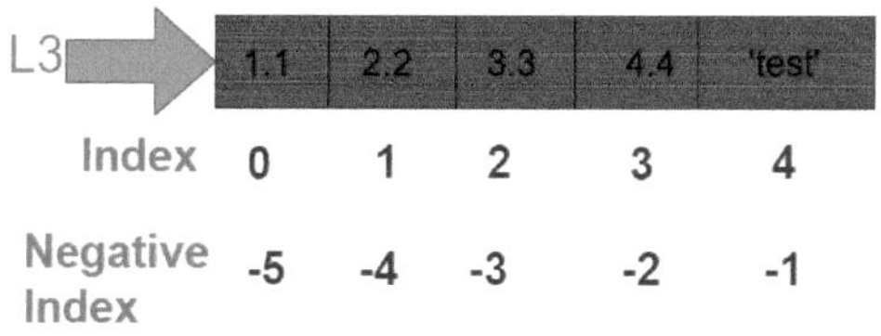

FIGURE 5.4 Negative index for different data types in the list.

Example:

```
# Python program to Print the length of the list
a = []
a.append("this")
a.append("is")
a.append("to")
a.append("test")
print("The length of list is: ", len(a))
```

Result

```
The length of list is: 4
```

The cited example prints the length of the list. The variable "a" is created with the empty list. To that empty list, first the string "this" was appended. Now the list contains one element, that is, a=["this"]. Next, three more strings are appended to the list – append means adding the content to the last of the existing list. After line 5 the list seems like a= ["this"," is"," to"," test"]. The length is the total number of the elements of the list. The predefined method len() returns the length of the list.

Example

```
#Accessing Elements in Reversed Order
systems = ['Windows', 'macOS', 'Linux']
# Printing Elements in Reversed Order
For o in reversed(systems):
print(o)
```

Result

```
Linux
macOS
Windows
```

The cited example reverses the elements of the list. The reversed () is the predefined method that reverses the sequence of the elements. The original sequence of the list is the Windows, MacOS, and Linux. After applying the reversed () on the list systems, the sequence becomes Linux, MacOS, and Windows.

Example

```
#program to swap any two elements in the list
# Getting list from user
myList = []
length = int(input("Enter number of elements: "))
for i in range(0, length):
val = int(input())
myList.append(val)
print("Enter indexes to be swapped")
index1 = int(input("index 1: "))
index2 = int(input("index 2: "))
print("Initial List: ", myList)
# Swapping given elements
myList[index1], myList[index2] = myList[index2],
myList[index1]
# printing list
print("List after Swapping: ", myList)
```

Result

```
Enter number of elements: 4
```

```
2
4
7
9
Enter indexes to be swapped
index 1: 1
index 2: 3
Initial List: [2, 4, 7, 9]
List after Swapping: [2, 9, 7, 4]
```

The cited example swaps the elements in the list. The list name myl-ist the list variable, and it is the empty list. The length consists of the count value, which the user wants to enter the number of values to the list. The user-entered value is stored in the variable val, and this variable is appended to the list mylist. Later swapped the index1 value with the index2 value.

Example

```
#Negative List Indexing In a Nested List
L = ['a', 'b', ['cc', 'dd', ['eee', 'fff']], 'g', 'h']
print(L[-3])
# Prints ['cc', 'dd', ['eee', 'fff']]
print(L[-3] [-1])
# Prints ['eee', 'fff']
print(L[-3] [-1] [-2])
```

Result

```
['cc', 'dd',['eee', 'fff']]
['eee', 'fff']
eee
```

The cited example retrieves the list elements using the negative index. The index – 1 represents the list element 'h' and – 2 represents the list ele-ment 'g', – 3 list element ['cc', 'dd', ['eee', 'fff']], – 4 list element 'b', and – 5 points to the list element 'a'. In line 4, L [-3] [-1] first retrieves the element ['cc', 'dd', ['eee', 'fff']] and later – 1 retrieves the element ['eee', 'fff']. L [-3] [-1] [-2] first retrieves the – 3 element ['cc', 'dd', ['eee', 'fff']] and later – 1 retrieves the element ['eee', 'fff']. In this list – 1 is 'fff' and – 2 is 'eee'. So L [-3] [-1] [-2] retrieves the element 'eee'.

5.5 UPDATING LIST

The Examplemers can update the single list or multiple list elements by providing the slice on the left-hand side of the assignment operator. The Examplemer can add up elements to the already existing list with the append () method.

Example

```
L1= ['this', 'is', 'to', 'test']
print(L1[0:3])
L1[1] ='testing'
print(L1[0:3])
```

Result

```
['this', 'is', 'to']
['this', 'testing', 'to']
```

In the cited example, L1[1]='testing' in line 2 replaces the string at L1[1] from 'is' to 'testing'.

Example

```
# Python program to demonstrate comparison
# between extend, insert and append
# assign lists
list_1 = [1, 2, 3]
list_2 = [1, 2, 3]
list_3 = [1, 2, 3]
a = [2, 3]
# use methods
list_1.append(a)
list_2.insert(3, a)
list_3.extend(a)
# display lists
print(list_1)
print(list_2)
print(list_3)
```

Result

```
[1, 2, 3, [2, 3]]
[1, 2, 3, [2, 3]]
[1, 2, 3, 2, 3]
```

In the cited example, the variable a is appended to the already existing list list_1. The contents of the list a is added to the last of the already existing list list_1. The list, after adding the variable a to the list list_1, becomes [1, 2, 3, [2, 3]]. The insert method adds the specific content at the specific location. At line 10, the variable a is inserted at the third location to the list list_2. After inserting the variable a to the list_2, the contents in list_2 are [1, 2, 3, [2, 3]]. The extend function adds the contents to the end of the list. After extending the list_3, the contents are [1, 2, 3, 2, 3].

5.6 DELETE LIST ELEMENTS

To remove the list elements, the Examplemer can use the del statement or the remove () method.

Example

```
L1=['this', 'is', 'to', 'test']
print(L1[0:4])
print(L1[3])
del(L1[3])
print(L1[0:3])
```

Result

```
['this', 'is', 'to', 'test']
test
['this', 'is', 'to']
```

In the cited example, del () method is used to delete the elements from the list. The statement del(L1[3]) deletes the index 3 element from the list, that is, the string test is deleted from the list L1.

5.7 SORTING

Sort the list is sorting the elements of the list, that is, arranging the elements in the list. The predefined methods sort () and sorted () are used to sort the list.

Example: sort the list elements

```
#Sort a given list
# vowels list
vowels = ['e', 'a', 'u', 'o', 'i']
# sort the vowels
```

```
vowels.sort()
# print vowels
print('sorted list: ', vowels)
```

Result

```
sorted list: ['a', 'e', 'i', 'o', 'u']
```

Example

```
# Python prog to illustrate the following in a list
def find_len(list1):
length = len(list1)
list1.sort()
print("Largest element is:", list1[length-1])
print("Smallest element is:", list1[0])
print("Second Largest element is:", list1[length-2])
print("Second Smallest element is:", list1[1])

# Driver Code
list1=[12, 45, 2, 41, 31, 10, 8, 6, 4]
Largest = find_len(list1)
```

Result

```
Largest element is : 45
Smallest element is: 2
Second Largest element is : 41
Second Smallest element is: 4
```

In the cited example, the list is sorted using the sort () function. After sorting the list, it displays the first largest element, second largest element, first smallest, and the second smallest element.

5.8 COPYING

The predefined method copy () returns the shallow copy of the list.

Example

```
#Copying a List
# mixed list
my_list = ['cat', 0, 6.7]
# copying a list
```

```
new_list = my_list.copy()
print('copied List:', new_list)
```

Result

```
Copied List: ['cat', 0, 6.7]
```

The cited example copies one complete list to another list. The pre-defined method copy copies the my_list elements to the list new_list.

Example

```
#Copy List Using Slicing Syntax
# shallow copy using the slicing syntax # mixed list
list = ['cat', 0, 6.7]
# copying a list using slicing
new_list = list[:]
# Adding an element to the new list
new_list.append('dog')
# Printing new and old list
print('Old List:', list)
print('New List:', new_list)
```

Result

```
Old List: ['cat', 0, 6.7]
New List: ['cat', 0, 6.7, 'dog']
```

In the cited example, the variable list contains three elements. The variable new_list copies the variable list elements, that is, it does not specify the index location, so it copies all the target list elements. A string 'dog' is appended to the new_list variable. The new_list contains the elements ['cat', 0, 6.7, 'dog'].

5.9 OPERATORS ON LISTS

The operators used for list are tabulated in Table 5.3

TABLE 5.3   Operators Used for List

Operator	Description
+	Concatenation
*	Repetition
In	Membership, iteration
not in	Not membership

Example

```
#Repetition operator on Strings
s1="python"
print (s1*3)
```

Result

```
pythonpythonpython
```

In the cited example, * works as the repetition operator. Print(s1*3) means s1 is repeated three times, so the string python is repeated three times.

Example

```
# membership operators in lists

# declare a list and a string
str1 = "Hello world"
list1 = [10, 20, 30, 40, 50]

# Check 'w' (capital exists in the str1 or not
if 'w' in str1:
      print("Yes! w found in ", str1)
else:
      print("No! w does not found in ", str1)
# check 'X' (capital) exists in the str1 or not
if 'X' not in str1:
      print("Yes! X dose not exist in ", str1)
else:
      print("No! X exists in ", str1)
# Check 30 exists in the list1 or not
if 30 in list1:
      print("Yes! 30 found in ", list1)
else:
      print("No! 30 does not found in ", list1)
# Check 90 exists in the list1 or not
if 90 not in list1:
      print("Yes! 90 dose not exist in ", list1)
else:
      print("No! 90 exist in ", list1)
```

Result

```
Yes! w found in Hello world
yes! X does not exist in Hello world
Yes! 30 found in [10, 20, 30, 40, 50]
Yes! 90 does not exist in [10, 20, 30, 40, 50]
```

In the cited example, the membership operator in is used to check whether the list element exists in the list or not. The statement 'w' in str1 means checking whether the character w exists in the string str1.

5.10 INDEXING, SLICING

A slice allows the Examplemer to make either a copy or part of the list.

Syntax

```
List name [start end]
List name [: end] ~ list name [0: end]
```

A slice of the list makes a new list, taking elements from the source list and the elements of the indices from start to end-1.

Note: Can use the negative values for both start and the end limits.

Example: Slicing

```
#whole list using slicing
# Initialize list
List = [1, 2, 3, 4, 5, 6, 7, 8, 9]

# Show original list
print("\nOriginal List:\n", List)

print("\nSliced List: ")

# Display sliced list
print(List[3:9:2])

# Display sliced list
print(List[::2])
```

```
# Display sliced list
print(List[::])
```

Result

```
Original List:
[1, 2, 3, 4, 5, 6, 7, 8, 9]

Sliced Lists:
[4, 6, 8]
[1, 3, 5, 7, 9]
[1, 2, 3, 4, 5, 6, 7, 8, 9]
```

In the cited example, the variable list consists of nine elements. The statement List [3:9:2] returns the elements starting from index 3, that is, index 3 element is 4, and last slice operator 2 indicates 2 steps increment (that is, the next element to retrieve is +2 element means index 3 + 2, so retrieves the index 5 element) retrieves the element 6, and it repeats up to last list index 9.

5.11 SEARCHING IN LIST

To perform the search operation on the list, the users have to perform the linear search. There is no predefined method to perform the search operation on the list.

```
#Largest and smallest element in the list
lst = []
num = int(input('How many numbers: '))
for n in range(num):
numbers = int(input('Enter number '))
lst.append(numbers)
print("Maximum element in the list is :", max(lst),
"\nMinimum element in the list is :", min(lst))
```

Result

```
How many numbers: 4
Enter number 1
Enter number 3
Enter number 5
Enter number 7
Maximum element in the list is : 7
Minimum element in the list is : 1
```

In the cited example, max () and min () are predefined methods to display the maximum and the minimum elements from the list.

```
#''' Python3 code for k largest elements in an list'''

def kLargest(arr, k):
# Sort the given array arr in reverse
# order.
arr.sort(reverse = True)
# Print the first kth largest elements
for i in range(k):
print (arr[i], end =" ")

# Driver program
arr = [1, 23, 12, 9, 30, 2, 50]
# n = len(arr)
k = 3
kLargest(arr, k)
```

Result

```
50 30 23
```

In the cited example, the max three elements are displaying. For this, first the array is sorted in the ascending order, and later the top three elements are used by using the for loop.

5.12 NESTED LIST

A list which in turn contains another list called the nested list. The nested list L1= [[1, 2, 3, 4], [5, 6], [7, 8, 9]]. Representation is shown in **Figure 5.5**.

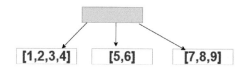

FIGURE 5.5 Nested list representation.

The negative index for the nested list is represented in **Figure 5.6**. L1=['A', 'B', [7, "test", 5.8], 25.5]

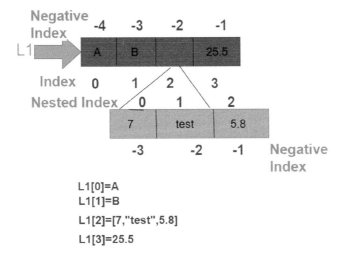

L1[0]=A
L1[1]=B
L1[2]=[7,"test",5.8]
L1[3]=25.5

FIGURE 5.6   Nested list negative index.

```
#2D list
a = [[1, 2, 3, 4], [5, 6], [7, 8, 9]]
for i in range(len(a)):
for j in range(len(a[i])):
print(a[i][j], end=' ')
print()
```

Result

```
1 2 3 4
5 6
7 8 9
```

In the cited example, the nested 2D list is presented. The outer list consists of only one element, and the inner list consists of three elements.

```
#Find Nested List length
L = ['a', ['bb', 'cc'], 'd']
print(len(L))
# Prints 3
print(len(L[1]))
```

Result

```
3
2
```

The cited examples display the length of the nested list. The outer list consists of three elements, and the inner list consists of two elements.

Nested list: 3D

```
#3D list
x = 2
y = 2
z = 2
a_3d_list = []

for i in range(x):
a_3d_list.append([])

for j in range(y):
a_3d_list[i].append([])

for k in range(z):
a_3d_list[i][j].append(0)
print(a_3d_list)
```

Result

```
[[[0, 0], [0, 0]], [[0, 0], [0,0]]]
```

5.13 LIST COMPREHENSION

List comprehension offers a short syntax to define and create a list based on the existing list.

Example: Nested list

```
#Nested List Comprehensions
matrix = []
for i in range(5):
# Append an empty sublist inside the list
Matrix.append([])
for j in range(5):
matrix[i].append(j)
print(matrix)
```

Result

```
[[0, 1, 2, 3, 4], [0, 1, 2, 3, 4], [0, 1, 2, 3, 4],
[0, 1, 2, 3, 4], [0, 1, 2, 3, 4]]
```

Example

```
# Nested list comprehension
matrix = [[j for j in range(5)] for i in range(5)]
print(matrix)
```

Result

```
[[0, 1, 2, 3, 4], [0, 1, 2, 3, 4], [0, 1, 2, 3, 4],
[0, 1, 2, 3, 4], [0, 1, 2, 3, 4]]
```

5.14 MATRIX REPRESENTATION

A matrix is a n-dimensional data structure where the data are arranged as the rows and the columns. The Python list can also be represented as the matrices.

Example

```
print ("enter first matrix size")
row=int (input ("enter row size "))
col=int (input ("enter column size "))
a= []
for i in range(row):
c= []
for j in range(col):
c.append(int(input("number:")))
a.append(c)
for i in range(row):
for j in range(col):
print(a[i][j],end=" ")
print()
```

Result

```
enter first matrix size
enter row size 2
```

```
enter column size 2
number:1
number:2
number:3
number:4
1 2
3 4
```

Lists can be represented as lists in the cited example. The variable 'a' is the empty list and all the user entered elements are stored in the list 'c'. Later the list 'c' is appended to the list 'a'.

Example

```python
print("enter first matrix elements")
row=int(input("enter row size "))
col=int(input("enter column size "))
a=[]
for i in range(row):
c=[]
for j in range(col):
c.append(int(input("number:")))
a.append(c)
for i in range(row):
for j in range(col):
print(a[i][j],end=" ")
print()
print("enter second matrix elements")
row1=int(input("enter row size "))
col1=int(input("enter column size "))
a1=[]
for i in range(row1):
c1=[]
for j in range(col1):
c1.append(int(input("number:")))
a1.append(c1)
for i in range(row1):
for j in range(col1):
print(a1[i][j],end=" ")
print()
print("Matrix Addition")
if row==row1 and col==col1:
```

```
for i in range(row1):
for j in range(col1):
print(a[i][j]+a1[i][j],end=" ")
print()
else:
print("addition not possible")
```

Result

```
enter first matrix elements
enter row size 2
enter column size 2
number:1
number:2
number:3
number:4
1 2
3 4
enter second matrix elements
enter row size 2
enter column size 2
number:5
number:6
number:7
number:8
5 6
7 8
Matrix Addition
6 8
10 12
```

The cited examples perform the matrix addition. The result shown is only for 2 × 2 matrix additions. The uses can try other than this row and column sizes.

Solved Examples

Example

```
# Python program to Print the length of the list
n = len([10, 20, 30])
print("The length of list is: ", n)
```

Result

```
The length of list is: 3
```

Example

```
# Python program to Print the length of the list
# Initializing list
test_list = [1, 4, 5, 7, 8]
# Printing test_list
print ("The list is : " + str(test_list))
# Finding length of list using loop Initializing
counter
counter = 0
for i in test_list:
# incrementing counter
counter = counter + 1
# Printing length of list
print ("Length of list using naive method is : " +
str(counter))
```

Result

```
The list is : [1, 4, 5, 7, 8]
Length of list using naive method is : 5
```

Example: Print the list in the reverse order

```
#Reverse a List
systems = ['Windows', 'macOS', 'Linux']
print('Original List:', systems)
# List Reverse
systems.reverse()
# updated list
print('Updated List:', system)
```

Result

```
Original List: ['Windows', 'macOS', 'Linux']
Updated List: ['Linux', 'macOS', 'Windows']
```

Example

```
#Reverse a List Using Slicing Operator
systems = ['Windows', 'macOS', 'Linux']
```

```
print('Original List:', systems)
# Reversing a list
#Syntax: reversed_list = systems[start:stop:step]
reversed_list = systems[::-1]
# updated list
print('Updated List:', reversed_list)
```

Result

```
Original List: ['Windows', 'macOS', 'Linux']
Updated List: ['Linux', 'macOS', 'Windows']
```

Example

```
#Swapping two values based on their values entered by
the user
# Getting list from user
myList = []
length = int(input("Enter number of elements: "))
for i in range(0, length):
val = int(input())
myList.append(val)
print("Enter values to be swapped ")
value1 = int(input("value 1: "))
value2 = int(input("value 2: "))
index1 = myList.index(value1)
index2 = myList.index(value2)
print("Initial List: ", myList)
# Swapping given element
myList[index1], myList[index2] = myList[index2],
myList[index1]
# Printing list
print("List after Swapping: ", myList)
```

Result

```
Enter number of elements: 4
1
3
4
5
Enter values to be swapped
value 1: 3
value 2: 5
```

```
Initial List: [1,3,4,5]
List after Swapping: [1, 5, 4, 3]
```

Example

```
#Python program to interchange first and last elements
in a list
# Swap function
def swapList(newList):
size = len(newList)
# Swapping
temp = newList[0]
newList[0] = newList[size - 1]
newList[size - 1] = temp
return newList
# list
newList = [12, 35, 9, 56, 24]
print(swapList(newList))
[24, 35, 9, 56, 12]
```

Example

```
#Swap the first and last elements is to use inbuilt
function list.pop().
# Swap function
def swapList(list):
first = list.pop(0)
last = list.pop(-1)
list.insert(0, last)
list.append(first)
return list
#list
newList = [12, 35, 9, 56, 24]
print(swapList(newList))
```

Result

```
[24, 35, 9, 56, 12]
```

Example

```
#Reverse the first half of list elements in python
l=list(map(int,input("Enter Number:").split()))
start=0
```

```
stop=len(l)//2 -1
while(start<stop):
l[start],l[stop]=l[stop],l[start]
start+=1
stop-=1
print(l)
```

Result

```
Enter Numbers:4
[4]
```

Example: append () and insert ()

```
#Inserting an Element to the List
# vowel list
vowel = ['a', 'e', 'i', 'u']
# 'o' is inserted at index 3 (4th position)
vowel.insert(3, 'o')
print('Updated List:', vowel)
```

Result

```
Updated List: ['a', 'e', 'i', 'o', 'u']
```

Example

```
#Inserting a Tuple (as an Element) to the List
mixed_list = [{1,2}, [5, 6, 7]]
# number tuple
number_tuple = (3, 4)
# inserting a tuple to the list
mixed_list.insert(1, number_tuple)
print('Updated List:', mixed_list)
```

Result

```
Updated List: [{1, 2}, (3, 4), [5, 6, 7]]
```

Example

```
# python program to demonstrate working of append
function
# assign list
l = ['pythom']
```

```
# use method
l.append('program')
l.append('course')
# display list
print(l)
```

Result

```
['pythom', 'program', 'course']
```

Example

```
#Nested List
L = ['a', 'b', ['cc', 'dd', ['eee', 'fff']], 'g', 'h']
print(L[2])
# Prints ['cc', 'dd', ['eee', 'fff']]
print(L[2][2])
# Prints ['eee', 'fff']
print(L[2][2][0])
# Prints eee
```

Result

```
['cc', 'dd', ['eee', 'fff']]
['eee', 'fff']
eee
```

Example

```
import functools
# filtering odd numbers
lst = filter(lambda x : x % 2 == 1, range(1,20))
print(lst)
# filtering odd square which are divisible by 5
lst = filter(lambda x : x % 5 == 0,
[x ** 2 for x in range(1,11) if x % 2 ==1])
print(lst)
# filtering negative numbers
lst = filter((lamba x: x < 0), range(-5,5))
print(lst)
# implementing max() function, using
print (functools.reduce(lambda a,b: a if (a > b) else
b, [7, 12, 45, 100, 15]))
```

Result

```
<filter object at 0x7f9ec4201f50>
<filter object at 0x7f9ec84b4410>
<filter object at 0x7f9ec4201f50>
100
```

Example 18

```
x= []
t=x [0]
print(t)
```

Result

```
IndexError   Traceback (most recent call last)
<ipython-input-12-a29e2cf34d86> in <module>()
1 x= []
- ----> 2 t=x [0]
3 print(t)
IndexError: list index out of range
- -------------------------
```

Example

```
# Python code to clone or copy a list Using the
in-built function list()
def Cloning(li1):
li_copy = li1
return li_copy
# list
li1 = [4, 8, 2, 10, 15, 18]
li2 = Cloning(li1)
print("Original List:", li1)
print("After Cloning:", li2)
```

Result

```
Original List: [4, 8, 2, 10, 15, 18]
After Cloning: [4, 8, 2, 10, 15, 18]
```

Example 36

```python
# python code to clone or copy a list Using list
comprehension
def Cloning(li1):
li_copy = [i for i in li1]
return li_copy
# list
li1 = [4, 8, 2, 10, 15, 18]
li2 = Cloning(li1)
print("Original List:", li1)
print("After Cloning:", li2)
```

Result

```
Original List: [4, 8, 2, 10, 15, 18]
After Cloning: [4, 8, 2, 10, 15, 18]
```

Example

```python
# python code to clone or copy a list Using append()
def closing(li1):
li_copy =[]
for item in li1: li_copy.append(item)
return li_copy
# list
li1 = [4, 8, 2, 10, 15, 18]
li2 = Cloning(li1)
print("Original List:", li1)
print("After Cloning:", li2)
```

Result

```
Original List: [4, 8, 2, 10, 15, 18]
After Cloning: [4, 8, 2, 10, 15, 18]
```

Example

```python
# python code to clone or copy a list Using bilt-in
method copy()
def Cloning(li1):
li_copy = []
li_copy = li1.copy()
return li_copy
```

```
# list
li1 = [4, 8, 2, 10, 15, 18]
li2 = Cloning(li1)
print("Original List:", li1)
print("After Cloning:", li2)
```

Result

```
Original List: [4, 8, 2, 10, 15, 18]
After Cloning: [4, 8, 2, 10, 15, 18]
```

Example: membership operators in lists

```
#members hip operators in and not in
a = 10
b = 20
list = [1, 2, 3, 4, 5] ;
if (a in list) :
print("Line 1 - a is available in the given list")
else:
print("Line 1 - a is not available in the given list")
if (b not in list) :
print("Line 2 - b is not available in the given list")
else:
print("Line 2 - b is available in the given list")
a = 2
if (a in list) :
print("Line 3 - a is available in the given list")
else:
print("Line 3 - a is not available in the given list")
```

Result

```
Line 1 - a is not available in the given list
Line 2 - b is not available in the given list
Line 3 - a is available in the given list
```

Example

```
# * Operator on lists
def multiply(a, b):
return a * b
values = [1, 2]
```

```
print(multiply(*values))
print(multiply(1,2))
```

Result

```
2
2
```

Example

```
#Repetition operator on lists
l1=[1,2,3]
print (l1 * 3)
```

Result

```
[1, 2, 3, 1, 2, 3, 1, 2, 3]
```

Example

```
#Repetition operator on a nested list
l1=[[2]]
l2=l1*2
print (l2)
l1[0][0]=99
print (l1)
print (l2)
```

Result

```
[[2], [2]]
[[99]]
[[99], [99]]
```

Example

```
#whole list using slicing
# Initialize list
Lst = [50, 70, 30, 20, 90, 10, 50]
# Display list
print(Lst[::])
```

Result

```
[50, 70, 30, 20, 90, 10, 50]
```

Example 49: negative slicing

```
#negative slicing
# Initialize list
Lst = [50, 70, 30, 20, 90, 10, 50]
# Display list
print(Lst[-7::1])
```

Result

```
[50, 70, 30, 20, 90, 10, 50]
```

Example 50

```
# Negative indexing in lists
my_list = ['p','r','o','b','e']
print(my_list[-1])
print(my_list[-5])
```

Result

```
e
p
```

Example: Delete part of the list using slicing

```
#Delete part of the list using slincing
l = [0, 1, 2, 3, 4, 5, 6, 7, 8, 9]
print(l)
# [0, 1, 2, 3, 4, 5, 6, 7, 8, 9]
del l[0]
print(l)
# [1, 2, 3, 4, 5, 6, 7, 8, 9]
del l[-1]
print(l)
# [1, 2, 3, 4, 5, 6, 7, 8]
del l[6]
print(l)
# [1, 2, 3, 4, 5, 6, 8]
```

Result

```
[0, 1, 2, 3, 4, 5, 6, 7, 8, 9]
[1, 2, 3, 4, 5, 6, 7, 8, 9]
[1, 2, 3, 4, 5, 6, 7, 8]
[1, 2, 3, 4, 5, 6, 8]
```

Example: Delete complete list using slicing

```
#Delete complete list using slincing
l = [0, 1, 2, 3, 4, 5, 6, 7, 8, 9]
del l[:]
print(l)
```

Result

```
[]
```

Example

```
#Change Nested List Item Value
L = ['a', ['bb', 'cc'], 'd']
L[1][1] = 0
print(L)
```

Result

```
['a', ['bb', 0], 'd']
```

Example

```
#Add items to a Nested list
L = ['a', ['bb', 'cc'], 'd']
L[1].append('xx')
print(L)
# Prints ['a', ['bb', 'cc', 'xx'], 'd']
```

Result

```
['a', ['bb', 'cc', 'xx'], 'd']
```

Example

```
#Insert items to a Nested list
L = ['a', ['bb', 'cc'], 'd']
L[1].insert(0, 'xx')
print(L)
```

Result

```
['a', ['xx', 'bb', 'cc'], 'd']
```

Example

```
#extend items to a Nested list
L = ['a', ['bb', 'cc'], 'd']
L[1].extend([1,2,3])
print(L)
# Prints ['a', ['bb', 'cc', 1, 2, 3], 'd']
```

Result

```
['a', ['bb', 'cc', 1, 2, 3], 'd']
```

Example

```
#Remove items from a Nested List
L = ['a', ['bb', 'cc', 'dd'], 'e']
x = L[1].pop(1)
print(L)
# removed item
print(x)
# Prints cc
```

Result

```
['a', ['bb', 'dd'], 'e']
cc
```

Example

```
#Remove items from a Nested List use the del
statement.
L = ['a', ['bb', 'cc', 'dd'], 'e']
del L[1][1]
print(L)
# Prints ['a', ['bb', 'dd'], 'e']
```

Result

```
['a', ['bb', 'dd'], 'e']
```

Example

```
#Remove items from a Nested List use remove() method
to delete it by value.
```

```
L = ['a', ['bb', 'cc', 'dd'], 'e']
L[1].remove('cc')
print(L)
# Prints ['a', ['bb', 'dd'], 'e']
```

Result

```
['a', ['bb', 'dd'], 'e']
```

Example

```
#Iterate through a Nested List
L = [[1, 2, 3],[4, 5, 6],[7, 8, 9]]
for list in L:
for number in list:
print(number, end=' ')
```

Result

```
1 2 3 4 5 6 7 8 9
```

Example

```
# * Operator on lists
def multiply(a, b):
return a * b
values = [1, 2]
print(multiply(*values))
print(multiply(1, 2))
```

Result

```
2
2
```

Example

```
#Strings are concatenated
s1="Welcome"
s2="to"
s3="python"
s4=s1+s2+s3
print (s4)
```

Result

```
Welcometopython
```

Example

```
#Repetition operator on Strings
s1="python"
print (s1*3)
```

Result

```
pythonpythonpython
```

Example

```
#Repetition operator on lists
l1=[1,2,3]
print (l1 * 3)
```

Result

```
[1, 2, 3, 1, 2, 3, 1, 2, 3]
```

Example

```
#Repetition operator on a nested list
l1=[[2]]
l2=l1*2
print (l2)
l1[0][0]=99
print (l1)
print (l2)
```

Result

```
[[2], [2]]
[[99]]
[[99], [99]]
```

Example

```
#whole list using slicing
# Initialize list
Lst = [50, 70, 30, 20, 90, 10, 50]
```

```
# Display list
print(Lst[::])
```

Result

```
[50, 70, 30, 20, 90, 10, 50]
```

Example

```
#negative slicing
# Initialize list
Lst = [50, 70, 30, 20, 90, 10, 50]
# Display list
print(Lst[-7::1])
```

Result

```
[50, 70, 30, 20, 90, 10, 50]
```

EXERCISE

1. Write a Python program to print only the second element of the student names list.

2. Write a Python program to print the maximum element in the list.

3. Write a Python program to remove duplicate elements in the list.

## CHAPTER 6

Tuple

A tuple is a collection of objects in sequence that is ordered and immutable. The main difference between list and the tuple is the tuples use the parentheses, whereas the list uses the square brackets. The tuples cannot be changed unlike lists. The tuple elements are separated by the comma operator. Tuple index starts with 0. The example for the tuple is as follows:

```
T1= ('this', 'is', 'to', 'test')
T2= ("this", "is", "to", "test")
T3= (1,2,3,4,5)
T4= (1.1,2.2,3.3,4.4)
```

6.1 TUPLE CREATION

The empty tuple is written as two parentheses with nothing:

```
T1= ()
```

If the tuple contains a single element, the programmer must include the comma operator even if the tuple contains a single element. For example:

```
T1= (1,)
```

Program

```
t=tuple((1,2,3))
print(t)
t1=tuple(("this","is","to","test"))
```

DOI: 10.1201/9781003414322-6

```
print(t1)
t2=tuple((1,2,3,3,("this","is","to","test","test")))
print(t2)
```

Output

```
(1, 2, 3)
('this', 'is', 'to', 'test')
(1, 2, 3, 3, ('this', 'is', 'to', 'test', 'test'))
```

The preceding program demonstrates the tuple creation using tuple ().

Program

```
t=tuple((1,2,3))
print(t)
t1=tuple(("this","is","to","test"))
print(t1)
t2=tuple((1,2,3,3,("this","is","to","test","test"),
["test",1]))
print(t2)
```

Output

```
(1, 2, 3)
('this', 'is', 'to', 'test')
(1, 2, 3, 3, ('this', 'is', 'to', 'test', 'test'),
['test', 1])
```

The preceding program demonstrates the tuple creation.

Python provides predefined functions for tuples. They are tabulated in Table 6.1, and predefined method for tuples are tabulated in Table 6.2.

TABLE 6.1   Predefined Functions for Tuples

Function	Description
cmp(tuple1, tuple2)	Compares the elements of the two tuples
len(tuple)	Gives the total length of the tuple
max(tuple)	Returns the max value of the tuple
min(tuple)	Returns min value of the tuple
tuple(sequence)	Converts the list to tuple

TABLE 6.2   Predefined Method for Tuple

Method	Description
count()	Returns the number of times a specified value occurs in a tuple
index()	Searches the tuple for a specified value and returns the position of where it was found

Program

```
t=tuple((1,2,3,3,"this","is","to","test","test",
["test",1]))
print(t.count(3))
print(t.count("test"))
print(t.index(3))
print(t.index("test"))
```

Output

```
2
2
2
7
```

The preceding program performs predefined methods of tuple.

6.2 ACCESSING VALUES IN TUPLES

To retrieve values in tuple, use either the index or indices inside the square bracket. For example:

```
T1=("this","is","to","test")
print(T1[0])
print(T1[0:3])
```

Output

```
this
('this', 'is', 'to')
```

Program

```
s=tuple(("this","is","to","test","python","tuple",
"example","collection","data","type"))
print(s)
```

```
print("s[:6]--",s[:6])
print("s[4:]--",s[4:])
print("s[-1]--",s[-1])
print("s[-2:]--",s[-2:])
print("s[-2:5]--",s[-2:5])
print("s[5:-2]--",s[5:-2])
print("s[::-1]--",s[::-1])
print("s[-10]--",s[-10])
print("s[-9]--",s[-9])
print("s[:-1]--",s[:-1])
print("s[5:-1]--",s[5:-1])
print("s[5:-2]--",s[5:-2])
print("s[-5:-2]--",s[-5:-2])
```

Output

```
('this', 'is', 'to', 'test', 'python', 'tuple',
  'example', 'collection', 'data', 'type')
s[:6]-- ('this', 'is', 'to', 'test', 'python', 'tuple')
s[4:]-- ('python', 'tuple', 'example', 'collection',
'data', 'type')
s[-1]-- type
s[-2:]-- ('data', 'type')
s[-2:5]-- ()
s[5:-2]-- ('tuple', 'example', 'collection')
s[::-1]-- ('type', 'data', 'collection', 'example',
'tuple', 'python', 'test', 'to', 'is', 'this')
s[-10]-- this
s[-9]-- is
s[:-1]-- ('this', 'is', 'to', 'test', 'python',
'tuple', 'example', 'collection', 'data')
s[5:-1]-- ('tuple', 'example', 'collection', 'data')
s[5:-2]-- ('tuple', 'example', 'collection')
s[-5:-2]-- ('tuple', 'example', 'collection')
```

The preceding program accesses tuple elements using index notation.

Program

```
t=tuple((1,2,3))
for x in t:
print(x)
t1=tuple(("this","is","to","test"))
```

```
for x in t1:
print(x)
t2=tuple((1,2,3,3,("this","is","to","test","test"),
["test",1]))
for x in t2:
print(x)
```

Output

```
1
2
3
this
is
to
test
1
2
3
3
('this', 'is', 'to', 'test', 'test')
['test', 1]
```

The preceding program accesses tuple elements.

Program

```
s=tuple(("this","is","to","test"))
print(s)
print(sorted(s))
print(sorted(s,reverse=True))
```

Output

```
('this', 'is', 'to', 'test')
['is', 'test', 'this', 'to']
['to', 'this', 'test', 'is']
```

The preceding program sorts tuple using the sorted function.

Program: sort tuple numbers

```
s=tuple((2,3,1,7,3,4,5,8,9))
print(s)
```

```
print(sorted(s))
print(sorted(s,reverse=True))
```

Output

```
(2,  3,  1,  7,  3,  4,  5,  8,  9)
[1,  2,  3,  3,  4,  5,  7,  8,  9]
[9,  8,  7,  5,  4,  3,  3,  2,  1]
```

The preceding program sorts tuple of numbers using the sorted function.

Program

```
t=(('t','h','i','s'))
print(".join(t))
```

Output

```
this
```

The preceding program converts tuple to string.

6.3 UPDATING TUPLES

Tuples are immutable, that is, the programmer cannot update or modify the tuples of tuple elements. The programmer is able to take the portions of current tuples to create the new tuples. For example:

```
T1=("this","is","to","test")
T2=(1,2,3,4,5)
T3=T1+T2
print(T3)
```

When the preceding code is executed, it produces the following result:

```
('this',  'is',  'to',  'test',  1,  2,  3,  4,  5)
```

Program

```
s=tuple(("this","is","to","test"))
print("s:",s)
s=list(s)
s.append("tuple")
```

```
s=tuple(s)
print(s)
```

Output

```
s: ('this', 'is', 'to', 'test')
('this', 'is', 'to', 'test', 'tuple')
```

The preceding program adds item to the tuple.

Program

```
t=tuple((1,2,3))
print(t)
print("concat",t+t)
print("replicate",t*3)
```

Output

```
(1, 2, 3)
concat (1, 2, 3, 1, 2, 3)
replicate (1, 2, 3, 1, 2, 3, 1, 2, 3)
```

The preceding program concats and replicates on tuples.

6.4 DELETE TUPLE ELEMENTS

Tuples are immutable, that is, deleting an individual tuple element is not feasible. The programmer can remove an entire tuple by using the del statement. For example:

```
T1=("this","is","to","test")
print(T1[0:3])
del(T1)
print(T1)
```

Output

```
('this', 'is', 'to')
-------------------------------------------------------------
NameError                Traceback (most recent call last)
<ipython-input-5-f29dc347d682> in <module>()
2 print(T1[0:3])
3 del(T1)
```

```
---->4 print(T1)
NameError: name 'T1' is not defined
```

Program

```
t=tuple((1,2,3))
print(t)
del t
```

Output

```
(1, 2, 3)
```

The preceding program removes complete tuple.

Program

```
t=tuple((1,2,3,3,"this","is","to","test","test",
["test",1]))
print(t)
t=list(t)
t.remove(3)
print(t)
t.remove("test")
print(t)
for x in t:
t.remove(x)
t=tuple(t)
print(t)
```

Output

```
(1, 2, 3, 3, 'this', 'is', 'to', 'test', 'test',
['test', 1])
[1, 2, 3, 'this', 'is', 'to', 'test', 'test',
['test', 1]]
[1, 2, 3, 'this', 'is', 'to', 'test', ['test', 1]]
(2, 'this', 'to', ['test', 1])
```

The preceding program removes the elements from the tuple.

6.5 OPERATIONS ON TUPLES

The + and * operators work like a concatenation and replication operation on tuples.

Note: The + operator joins tuples together, and * operator multiplies tuples.

Program

```
t=(1, 2, 3)
t1=(4, 5, 6)
print(t+t1)
```

Output

```
(1, 2, 3, 4, 5, 6)
```

The preceding program performs + operator in tuples.

Program

```
t=(1, 2, 3)
t1=('test')
print(t+t1)
```

Output

```
----------------------------------------------------------------
TypeError            Traceback (most recent call last)
  <ipython-input-4-d4200773bff6> in <module>()
1 t=(1, 2, 3)
2 t1=('test')
----> 3 print(t+t1)
TypeError: can only concatenate tuple (not "str") to
  tuple
```

The preceding program performs + operator in integer and string tuples.

Program

```
t=(1, 2, 3)
print(t*3)
```

Output

```
(1, 2, 3, 1, 2, 3, 1, 2, 3)
```

The preceding program performs * operator in integer tuples.

Program

```
t1=('test')
print(t1*3)
```

Output

```
testtesttest
```

The preceding program performs * operator in string tuples.

⏰ **Note**: + operator works as the concatenation operator for tuples, and * operator works as the repetition operator for tuples.

Program

```
s=tuple(("this","is","to","test",(1,2,3),("true",
"false"),"1"))
print("s:",s)
print("this in s:", "this" in s)
print("3 in s:",3 in s)
print("false in s:","false" in s)
print("(1,2,3) in s:",(1,2,3) in s)
print("(1,2) in s:",(1,2) in s)
print("(1,2) not in s:",(1,2) not in s)
```

Output

```
s: ('this', 'is', 'to', 'test', (1, 2, 3), ('true',
'false'), '1')
this in s: True
3 in s: False
false in s: False
(1,2,3) in s: True
(1,2) in s: False
(1,2) not in s: True
```

The preceding program performs membership operators in tuple.

Program

```
s=tuple((1,2,3,4,5,6,9))
print(len(s))
print(max(s))
```

```
print(min(s))
print(sum(s))
```

Output

```
7
9
1
30
```

The preceding program performs aggregate operations on tuple.

Program

```
s=tuple((1,2,3,4))
s1=tuple((1,2,3))
print("s:",s)
print("s1:",s1)
print("s==s1:",s==s1)
print("s!=s1",s!=s1)
print("s<s1:",s<s1)
print("s>s1:",s>s1)
print("s>=s1:",s>=s1)
print("s<=s1:",s<=s1)
```

Output

```
s: (1, 2, 3, 4)
s1: (1, 2, 3)
s==s1: False
s!=s1 True
s<s1: False
s>s1: True
s>=s1: True
s<=s1: False
```

The preceding program performs comparison operators on tuples.

Program

```
# Tuple Largets and Smallest Item

lgsmTuple = (25, 17, 33, 89, 77, 10, 64, 11, 55)
print("Tuple Items = ", lgsmTuple)
```

```
tupLargest = lgsmTuple[0]
tupSmallest = lgsmTuple[0]
for i in range(len(lgsmTuple)):
  if(tupLargest < lgsmTuple[i]):
   tupLargest = lgsmTuple[i]
   tupLargestPos = i
  if(tupSmallest > lgsmTuple[i]):
   tupSmallest = lgsmTuple[i]
   tupSmallestPos = i

print("Largest Item in lgsmTuple Tuple = ",
  tupLargest)
print("Largest Tuple Item index Position = ",
  tupLargestPos)

print("Smallest Item in lgsmTuple Tuple = ",
  tupSmallest)
print("Smallest Tuple Item index Position = ",
  tupSmallestPos)
```

Output

```
Tuple Items =     (25, 17, 33, 89, 77, 10, 64, 11, 55)
Largest Item in lgsmTuple Tuple          =      89
Largest Tuple Item index Position   =      3
Smallest Item in lgsmTuple Tuple         =      10
Smallest Tuple Item index Position  =      5
```

6.6 UNPACKING OF TUPLES

In Python packing means placing a value in a new tuple, and unpacking means extracting the tuple values back to the variables.

Packing:

T=('this','is','to','test') # packing

Unpacking:

Mapping the right-hand arguments to the left-hand arguments. The total number of variables on the left-hand side should be equal to the total number of values in the tuple. For arbitrary length, use the * arguments.

e.g.: (a,b,c,d)=T # unpacking

Program

```
s=("this","is","to","test",(1,2,3),("true",
"false"), "1")
(a,b,c,d,e,f,g)=s
print(a)
print(b)
print(c)
print(d)
print(e)
print(f)
print(g)

print("Unpacking-1")
(a,b,*c)=s
print(a)
print(b)
print(c)

print("Unpacking-2")
(a,*b,c)=s
print(a)
print(b)
print(c)

print("Unpacking-3")
(*a,b,c)=s
print(a)
print(b)
print(c)
```

Output

```
this
is
to
test
(1, 2, 3)
('true', 'false')
1
Unpacking-1
this
is
```

```
['to', 'test', (1, 2, 3), ('true', 'false'), '1']
Unpacking-2
this
['is', 'to', 'test', (1, 2, 3), ('true', 'false')]
1
Unpacking-3
['this', 'is', 'to', 'test', (1, 2, 3)]
('true', 'false')
1
```

The preceding program performs unpacking the tuple.

6.7 INDEXING, SLICING ON TUPLES

The [] operator is used to index or slice the tuple in Python. Indexing the tuple uses either the positive or the negative value. The positive index fetches the index from the tuple left, whereas the negative index fetches from the tuple right. Tuple slicing uses the slicing operator (:) to retrieve a range of items.

Syntax for tuple index

```
Tuplename[index]
Syntax for tuple slicing
Tuplename[start:stop:step]
```

Program

```
t = ('a', 'b', 'c', 'd')
print(t[1])
print(t[-1])
print(t[:2])
print(t[1:3])
print(t[::2])
```

Output

```
b
d
('a', 'b')
('b', 'c')
('a', 'c')
```

The preceding program performs the tuple index and slicing on characters.

Program

```
t = (1,2,3,4)
print(t[1])
print(t[-1])
print(t[:2])
print(t[1:3])
print(t[::2])
```

Output

```
2
4
(1, 2)
(2, 3)
(1, 3)
```

The preceding program performs the tuple index and slicing on numbers.

Nested Tuple

Nested tuple is the tuple inside another tuple.

Program

```
s=tuple(("this","is","to","test",(1,2,3),("true",
"false"),"1"))
print(s[4])
print(s[4][0])
print(s[4][1])
print(s[4][2])
print(s[5])
print(s[5][0])
print(s[5][1])
```

Output

```
(1, 2, 3)
```

```
1
2
3
('true', 'false')
true
false
```

The preceding program performs accessing elements from the nested tuple.

Program

```
s=tuple("this","is","to","test",[1,2,3],["true",
"false"],"1"))
s[4][1]="test"
print(s)
s[5][0]="boolean"
print(s)
```

Output

```
('this', 'is', 'to', 'test', [1, 'test', 3], ['true',
  'false'], '1')
('this', 'is', 'to', 'test', [1, 'test', 3],
  ['boolean', 'false'], '1')
```

The preceding program modifies the nested tuple elements.

EXERCISE

1. Unpack a tuple with seven different types of elements.

2. Convert a tuple to string.

3. Retrieve the repeated elements of the tuple.

4. Convert a list to a tuple.

5. Find the length of the tuple.

6. Reverse the tuple.

7. Convert a tuple to dictionary.

8. Compute the sum of all the elements of the tuple.

## CHAPTER 7

Sets

7.1 INTRODUCTION

A set is a collection that is unordered and unindexed. In Python, sets are written with curly brackets.

```
S={"this", "is", "to", "test"}
```

There are two ways to create a set in Python.

1. Using curly brackets
2. Using set constructor

Syntax for curly brackets set creation

```
setname={"item1","item2", . . .}
```

Syntax using set constructor

```
Setname=set((={"item1","item2", . . .))
```

Program: creating the set

```
s={"this","is","to","test"}
print(s)
s1=set(("this","is","to","test"))
print(s1)
```

DOI: 10.1201/9781003414322-7

Output

```
{'test','is','to','this'}
{'test','is','to','this'}
```

Program: creating set with multiple data types

```
s={"this is to test",(1,2,3),("pyhton","set",
  "example"),10.34567}
print(s)
s1=set(("this is to test",(1,2,3),("pyhton","set",
  "example"),10.34567))
print(s1)
print("pyhton elements")
for x in s:
  print(x)
```

Output

```
{'this is to test', ('pyhton', 'set', 'example'),
  10.34567, (1, 2, 3)}
{'this is to test', ('pyhton', 'set', 'example'),
  10.34567, (1, 2, 3)}
Pyhton elements
this is to test
('pyhton', 'set', 'example')
10.34567
(1, 2, 3)
```

Program: giving duplicate values to the set

```
s={1,2,3,2,"this","is","to","test","test"}
print(s)
s1=set((1,2,3,2,"this","is","to","test","test"))
print(s1)
s2={(1,2,3,2),("this","is","to","test","test")}
Print(s2)
```

Output

```
{1, 2, 3, 'to', 'test', 'this', 'is'}
{1, 2, 3, 'to', 'test', 'this', 'is'}
{('this', 'is', 'to', 'test', 'test'), (1, 2, 3, 2)}
```

7.2 ACCESS SET ELEMENTS

The set items cannot be accessed by referring the index or the key.

The programmer has to use the loop to access the set elements.

Program: Access set items

```
s={"this", "is", "to", "test"}
print(s)
for x in s:
  print(x)
```

Output

```
{'test', 'is', 'to', 'this'}
test
is
to
this
```

7.3 ADDING ELEMENTS TO THE SET

To add the elements in the set, there is a predefined method called the add (). To add multiple items to the set, there is a predefined method called the update ().

Program: Adding elements to the set

```
s={"this","is","to","test"}
print(s)
s.add("pyhton")
print(s)
s.add("set")
print(s)
s.add("example")
print(s)
```

Output

```
{'test', 'is', 'to', 'this'}
{'this', 'to', 'pyhton', 'test', 'is'}
{'this', 'to', 'pyhton', 'set', 'test', 'is'}
{'this', 'example', 'to', 'pyhton', 'set', 'test',
  'is'}
```

Program: adding multiple items

```
s={"this","is","to","test"}
print(s)
s.update(["python","set","example"])
print(s)
```

Output

```
{'test', 'is', 'to', 'this'}
{'python', 'this', 'example', 'to', 'set', 'test', 'is'}
```

7.4 REMOVE AN ELEMENT FROM THE SET

To remove an element from the set, there are two predefined methods called the remove (), discard (). There is another predefined method called the pop () to remove the topmost element from the set. There is no guarantee that by using pop () which element from the set will be removed.

Program: Remove an element from the set

```
s={"this","is","to","test"}
print(s)
s.remove("test")
print(s)
s.discard("this")
print(s)
s.pop()
print(s)
```

Output

```
{'test', 'is', 'to', 'this'}
{'is', 'to', 'this'}
{'is', 'to'}
{'to'}
```

7.5 DELETE THE SET

There are two predefined methods called the clear () and del to delete the set elements. Clear only deletes the set elements and the empty set retains, but the del keyword deletes the entire set.

Program: using del keyword

```
s={"this","is","to","test"}
```

```
print(s)
s.clear()
print(s)
del s
```

Output

```
{'test', 'is', 'to', 'this'}
Set()
```

7.6 PYTHON SET OPERATIONS

Most of the set operations works on two sets. Table 7.1 tabulates the operations on sets.

TABLE 7.1   Python Set Operations

Operation	Symbol	Description
union	U	Combines both sets
intersection	∩	Selects elements that are common in both sets
difference	-	The elements in first set but not in second

Program: Set operations

```
s={1,2,3,"test"}
s1={"this","is","to","test","1",1}
print("s:",s)
print("s1:",s1)
print("s|s1:",s|s1)
print("s&s1:",s&s1)
print("s^s1:",s^s1)
print("s-s1:",s-s1)
print("s1-s:",s1-s)
```

Output

```
s: {1, 2, 3, 'test'}
s1: {1, 'this', '1', 'to', 'test', 'is'}
s|s1: {1, 2, 3, 'this', '1', 'to', 'test', 'is'}
s&s1: {1, 'test'}
s^s1: {2, 'is', 3, 'this', '1', 'to'}
s-sl: {2, 3}
s1-s: {'1', 'is', 'to', 'this'}
```

7.7 SET MEMBERSHIP OPERATORS

Set membership operators in Python test for membership in set. Table 7.2 tabulates the Python membership operations.

TABLE 7.2 Python Membership Operations

Operation	Description
in	Returns true if the element is found in the set; otherwise false
not in	Returns true if the element is not found in the set; otherwise false

Program: Set membership operators

```python
s={1,2,3,"test"}
print("s:",s)
print("test in s:","test" in s)
print("1 in s:"1 in s)
print("5 in s :",5 in s)
print("5 not in s",5 not in s)
```

Output

```
s: {1, 2, 3, 'test'}
test in s: True
1 in s: True
5 in s: False
5 not in s True
```

Program: Sort the set

```python
s={"this","is","to","test"}
print(s)
print(sorted(s))
print(sorted(s,reverse=True))
```

Output

```
{'test', 'is', 'to', 'this'}
['is', 'test', 'this', 'to']
['to', 'this', 'test', 'is']
```

7.8 SET PREDEFINED METHODS

Table 7.3 tabulates the set predefined methods in Python.

TABLE 7.3   Predefined Set Methods

Method	Description
add()	Adds an element to the set. Set maintains only unique elements; if the newly added element already exists in the set, then it does not add that element.
clear()	Removes all elements from the set.
copy()	Copies the set.
difference()	Returns the first set elements only that were not exist in the second set.
intersection()	Returns the elements that were common in the given sets.
pop()	Removes the random element from the set.
symmetric difference()	Returns the distinct elements that were found in the given sets.
union()	Combines the given sets.
update()	Updates the set by adding distinct elements from the passed ones.

Program: Set predefined functions

```
s={"this","is","to","test"}
s1={"this","is","to","test","1",1}
print("s:",s)
print("s1:",s1)
print("union:",s.union(s1))
print("intersection:",s.intersection(s1))
print("difference s-s1:",s.difference(s1))
print("difference s1-s:",s1.difference(s))
print("symmetric_difference s-s1:",
  s.symmetric_difference(s1))
print("symmetric_difference s1-s:",
  s1.symmetric_difference(s))
```

Output

```
s: {'test', 'is', 'to', 'this'}
s1: {1, 'this', '1', 'to', 'test', 'is'}
union: {1, 'this', '1', 'to', 'test', 'is'}
intersection: {'this', 'is', 'to', 'test'}
difference s-s1: set()
difference s1-s: {'1', 1}
```

```
symmetric_difference s-s1: {1, '1'}
symmetric_difference s1-s: {1, '1'}
```

Program: operation on 3 sets

```
s={"this","is","to","test"}
s1={"this","is","to","test","1",1}
s2=={1,2,3,2,"this","is","to","test","test"}
print("s:",s)
print("s1:",s1)
print("s2:",s2)
print("union:",s.union(s1,s2))
  print("intersection:",s.intersection(s1,s2))
  print("difference s-s1:",s.difference(s1,s2))
  print("difference s1-s:",s1.difference(s,s2))
```

Output

```
s: {'test', 'is', 'to', 'this'}
s1: {1, 'this', '1', 'to', 'test', 'is'}
s2: {('this', 'is', 'to', 'test', 'test'), (1, 2, 3, 2)}
union: {1, 'this', '1', 'to', ('this', 'is', 'to',
  'test','test'), 'test', (1, 2, 3, 2), 'is'}
intersection: set()
difference s-s1: set()
difference s1-s: {'1', 1}
```

Program: Operations on four sets

```
s={"this","is","to","test"}
s1={"this","is","to","test","1",1}
s2=={1,2,3,2,"this","is","to","test","test"}
s3={"this is to test",(1,2,3),("pyhton","set",
  "example"),10.34567}
print("s:",s)
print("s1:",s1)
print("s2:",s2)
print("s3:",s3)
print("union:",s.union(s1,s2,s3))
  print("intersection:",s.intersection(s1,s2,s3))
print("difference s-(s1,s2,s3):",
  s.difference(s1,s2,s3))
print("difference s1-(s,s2,s3):",
  s1.difference(s,s2,s3))
```

```
print("difference s2-(s1,s,s3):",
  s2.difference(s,s1,s3))
print("difference s3-(s1,s2,s):",
  s3.difference(s,s1,s2))
```

Output:

```
s: {'test', 'is', 'to', 'this'}
s1: {1, 'this', '1', 'to', 'test', 'is'}
s2: {('this', 'is', 'to', 'test', 'test'), (1, 2, 3, 2)}
s3: {'this is to test', ('pyhton', 'set', 'example'),
  10.34567, (1, 2, 3)}

union: {1, ('pyhton', 'set', 'example'), (1, 2, 3, 2),
  'to', 'this', 10.34567, (1, 2, 3), 'is', 'test',
  'this is to test', '1', ('this', 'is', 'to', 'test',
  'test')}
intersection: set()
difference s-(s1,s2,s3): set()
difference s1-(s,s2,s3): {1, '1'}
difference s2-(s1,s,s3): {(1, 2, 3, 2), ('this', 'is',
  'to', 'test', 'test')}
difference s3-(s1,s2,s): {10.34567, (1, 2, 3), 'this
  is to test', ('pyhton', 'set', 'example')}
```

Program: Relational operators on sets

```
S=(1,2,3,4)
S1=(l,2,3)
Print("s:",s)
print("s1:",s1)
print{"s==s1",s==s1)
print("s!=s1",s!=s1)
print("s<s1:",s<s1)
print{"s>s1:",s>s1)
print("s>=s1:",s>=s1)
print("s<=s1:",S<=sl)
```

Output

```
s: (1, 2, 3, 4)
s1: (1, 2, 3)
s==s1: False
s!=s1 True
s<s1: False
```

```
s>s1: True
s>=s1: True
s<=s1: False
```

Program: Intersection and difference

```
s={"this","is","to","test"}
s1={"this","is","to","test","1",1}
print("s:",s)
print("s1:",s1)
print("intersection:",s.intersection_update(s1))
print("difference s-(s1):",s.difference_update(s1))
print("difference s1-(s):",s1.difference_update(s))
print("Symmetric_difference s-(s1):",s.
  symmetric_difference_update(s1))
print("Symmetricdifference s1-(s):",s1.
  symmetric_differance_update(s))
```

Output

```
s: {'test', 'is', 'to', 'this'}
s1: {1, 'this', '1', 'to', 'test', 'is'}
intersection: None
difference s-(s1): None
difference s1-(s): None
Symmetric_difference s-(s1): None
Symmetricdifference s1-(s): None
```

7.9 FROZEN SET

A frozen set function returns an immutable frozen set object initialized with elements from the given object, like list, tuple, etc.

Syntax

frozenset(object), where object is the object of list, tuple etc.

Program 17: Creating frozen set

```
s=forzenset(("this","is","to","test"))
print(s)
```

Output

```
frozenset({'test', 'is', 'to', 'this'})
```

7.10 FROZEN SET OPERATIONS

Table 7.4 tabulates different frozen set operations in Python.

TABLE 7.4   Python Frozen Set Operations

Operation	symbol	Description
union	|	Combines both sets
intersection	&	Selects elements that are common in both sets
difference	-	The elements in first set but not in second

Program: Frozen set operations

```
s=frozenset(("this","is","to","test"))
s1=frozenset(("this","is","to","test","1",1))
print("s:",s)
print("s1:",s1)
print("s|s1:",s|s1)
print("s&s1:",s&s1)
print("s^s1:",s^s1)
print("s-s1:"s-s1)
print("s1-s:",s1-s)
```

Output

```
s: frozenset({'test', 'is', 'to', 'this'})
s1: frozenset({1, 'this', '1', 'to', 'test', 'is'})
s|s1: frozenset({1, 'this', '1', 'to', 'test', 'is'})
s&s1: frozenset({'this', 'is', 'to', 'test'})
s^s1: frozenset({1, '1'})
s-s1: frozenset()
s1-s: frozenset({'1', 1})
```

7.11 FROZEN SET PREDEFINED OPERATIONS

Table 7.5 tabulates the frozen set predefined operations.

TABLE 7.5   Frozen Set Predefined Operations

Method	Description
difference()	Returns the first set elements only that were not existing in the second set
intersection()	Returns the elements that were common in the given sets
symmetric_ difference()	Returns the distinct elements that were found in the given sets
union()	Combines the given sets

Program 18: frozen set predefined operations

```
s=frozenset(("this","is","to","test"))
s1=frozenset(("this","is","to","test","1",1))
print("s:",s)
print("s1:",s1)
print("union:",s.union(s1))
print("intersection:",s.intersection(s1))
print("difference s-s1:",s.difference(s1))
print("difference s1-s: ",s1.difference(s))
print("symmetric_difference s-s1: ",
  s.symmetric_difference(s1))
print("symmetric_difference s1-s: ",
  s1. symmetric_difference(s))
```

Output

```
s: frozenset({'test', 'is', 'to', 'this'})
s1: frozenset({1, 'this', '1', 'to', 'test', 'is'})
union: frozenset({1, 'this', '1', 'to', 'test', 'is'})
intersection: frozenset({'this', 'is', 'to', 'test'})
difference s-s1: frozenset()
difference s1-s: frozenset({'1', 1})
symmetric_difference s-s1: frozenset({1, '1'})
symmetric_difference s1-s: frozenset({1, '1'})
```

Program 19: Relational operators on frozen sets

```
s=frozenset((1,2,3,4))
s1=frozenset((1,2,3))
print("s:",s)
print("s1:",s1)
print("s==s1:"s==s1)
print{"s!=s1",s!=s1)
print("s<s1:",s<s1)
print("s>s1:",s>s1)
print("s>=s1:",s>=s1)
print("s<=s1:",s<=s1)
```

Output

```
s: frozenset({1,2,3,4})
s1: frozenset({1,2,3})
```

```
s==s1: False
s!=s1 True
s<s1: False
s>s1: True
s>=s1: True
s<=s1: False
```

Program 20: Operation on four frozen sets

```
s=frozenset(("this","is","to","test"))
s1=frozenset(("this","is","to","test","1",1))
s2==frozenset((1,2,3,2,"this","is","to","test","test"))
s3=frozenset(("this is to test",{1,2,3},("pyhton",
  "set","example"),10.34567))
print("s:",s)
print("s1:",s1)
print("s2:",s2)
print("s3:",s3)
print("union:",s.union(s1,s2,s3))
print("intersection:",s.intersection(s1,s2,s3))
print("difference s-(s1,s2,s3):",s.
  difference(s1,s2,s3))
print("difference s1-(s,s2,s3):",s1.
  difference(s,s2,s3))
print("difference s2-(s1,s,s3):",s2.
  difference(s,s1,s3))
print("difference s3-(s1,s2,s):",s3.
  difference(s,s1,s2))
```

Output

```
s: frozenset({'to', 'test', 'this', 'is'})
s1: frozenset({1, 'to', 'this', 'is', 'test', '1'})
s2: {(1, 2, 3, 2), ('this', 'is', 'to', 'test',
  'test')}
s3: frozenset({10.34567, (1, 2, 3), 'this is to test',
  ('pyhton', 'set', 'example')})
union: frozenset({1, ('pyhton', 'set', 'example'), (1,
  2, 3, 2), 'to', 'this', 10.34567, (1, 2, 3), 'is',
  'test', 'this is to test', '1', ('this', 'is', 'to',
  'test', 'test')})
intersection: frozenset()
difference s-(s1, s2,s3): frozenset()
```

```
difference s1-(s, s2, s3): frozenset({1, '1'})
difference s2-(s1, s, s3): {(1, 2, 3, 2), ('this',
  'is', 'to', 'test', 'test')}
difference s3-(s1, s2, s): frozenset({10.34567, (1, 2,
  3), 'this is to test', ('pyhton', 'set', 'example')})
```

Program 21: operation on 3 frozen sets

```
s=frozenset(("this","is","to","test"))
s1=frozenset(("this","is","to","test","1",1))
s2==frozenset((1,2,3,2,"this","is","to","test","test"))
print("s:",s)
print("s1:",s1)
print("s2:",s2)
print("union:",s.union(s1,s2))
print{"intersection:",s.intersection(s1,s2))
print{"difference s-(s1,s2):",s.difference(s1,s2))
print{"difference s1-(s,s2):",s1.difference(s,s2))
print{"difference s2-(s1,s):",s2.difference(s,s1))
```

Output

```
s: frozenset({'to', 'test', 'this', 'is'})
s1: frozenset({1, 'to', 'this', 'is', 'test', '1'})
s2: {(1, 2, 3, 2), ('this', 'is', 'to', 'test',
  'test')}
union: frozenset({1, (1, 2, 3, 2), 'to', 'this', 'is',
  'test', '1', ('this', 'is', 'to', 'test', 'test')})
intersection: frozenset()
difference s-(s1, s2): frozenset()
difference s1-(s, s2): frozenset({1, '1'})
difference s2-(s1, s): {(1, 2, 3, 2), ('this', 'is',
  'to', 'test', 'test')}
```

EXERCISE

1. Perform the union and the intersection operations on the set.

2. Verify whether the set is the subset of another set.

3. Remove all elements from the set and the frozen set.

4. Compare two sets.

5. Find the max and min elements from the set and the frozen set.

## CHAPTER 8

Dictionary

Dictionary is a Python data structure, and it is a set of key value pairs.

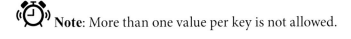 **Note**: Each key must be unique. It may be any type, and keys are case sensitive.

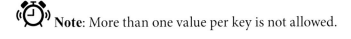 **Note**: More than one value per key is not allowed.

Empty dictionaries are constructed by an empty pair of curly braces, that is, {}.

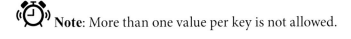 **Note**: By default, dictionaries are ordered collections.

In dictionary, each key is separated from its value by a colon (:), the items are separated by the comma operator, and both the keys and values are enclosed by curly braces.

Access the dictionary values

Syntax

```
dictionaryname[key]
```

Program

```
marks = {'java': 80, 'python': 90, 'ruby': 86}
print(list(marks)[0])
```

DOI: 10.1201/9781003414322-8

```
print(list(marks)[1])
print(list(marks)[2])
print(marks['java'])
```

Output

```
java
python
ruby
80
```

The preceding program accesses key elements. The dictionary name in this program is marks, and it consists of three elements. The keys in the marks dictionary are java, python, and ruby, and the corresponding values for the specified keys are 80, 90, and 86. To access the dictionary value, use the dictionary and its key value, that is, to access the java value from the marks dictionary, use marks['java'].

Program

```
marks = {'java': 80, 'python': 90, 'ruby': 86}
if "java" in marks:
print("Exists")
else:
print("Does not exist")
```

Output

```
Exists
```

The preceding program checks the existence of the key using the membership operators.

Program

```
marks = {'java': 80, 'python': 90, 'ruby': 86}
print("java" in marks)
print("c" not in marks)
```

Output

```
True
True
```

The preceding program checks membership operators with dictionaries.

Program

```
test= ('a', 'b', 'c')
dict = dict.fromkeys(test)
print("New Dictionary : %s" % str(dict))

dict = dict.fromkeys(test, 11)
print ("New Dictionary : %s" % str(dict))
```

Output

```
New Dictionary : {'a': None, 'b': None, 'c': None}
New Dictionary : {'a': 11, 'b': 11, 'c': 11}
```

The preceding program accesses dictionary using keys ().

Program

```
marks = {'java': 80, 'python': 90, 'ruby': 86}
print(sorted(marks.keys()))
print(sorted(marks.items()))
```

Output

```
['java', 'python', 'ruby']
[('java', 80), ('python', 90), ('ruby', 86)]
```

The preceding program accesses dictionary using sorted ().

Program

```
marks = {'java': 80, 'python': 90, 'ruby': 86}
print("Value : %s" % marks.items())
```

Output

```
Value : dict_items([('java', 80), ('python', 90),
  ('ruby', 86)])
```

The preceding program accesses dictionary using items ().

Program

```
marks = {'java': 80, 'python': 90, 'ruby': 86}
print("Value : %s" % marks.values())
```

Output

```
Value : dict_values([80, 90, 86])
```

The preceding program accesses dictionary using values ().

Program

```
marks = {'java': 80, 'python': 90, 'ruby': 86}
new = "JAVA"
old = "java"
marks[new] = marks.pop(old)

print(marks)
```

Output

```
{'python': 90, 'ruby': 86, 'JAVA': 80}
```

The preceding program modifies a key and items in dictionary.

Program

```
marks = {'java': 80, 'python': 90, 'ruby': 86}
print(marks.pop("ruby",None))
print(marks)
```

Output

```
  86
{'java': 80, 'python': 90}
```

The preceding program removes key from dictionary.

Program

```
marks = {'java': 80, 'python': 90, 'ruby': 86}
print(marks)
marks['pascal']=99
print(marks)
```

Output

```
{'java': 80, 'python': 90, 'ruby': 86}
{'java': 80, 'python': 90, 'ruby': 86, 'pascal': 99}
```

The preceding program inserts keys and items in the dictionary.

Program

```
marks = {'java': 80, 'python': 90, 'ruby': 86}
print(marks)
marks.update({'pascal':99})
print(marks)
```

Output

```
{'java': 80, 'python': 90, 'ruby': 86}
{'java': 80, 'python': 90, 'ruby': 86, 'pascal': 99}
```

The preceding program inserts keys and items in the dictionary using update ().

Program

```
a = [1, 2, 3, 4, 5, 6, 7, 8, 9, 10]
x = {n: n*n for n in a}
print(x)
```

Output

```
{1: 1, 2: 4, 3: 9, 4: 16, 5: 25, 6: 36, 7: 49, 8: 64,
 9: 81, 10: 100}
```

The preceding program converts list to dictionary.

Program

```
d={'id':1,'name':'usharani','age':33,'id':5}
print(d['id'])
```

Output

```
5
```

The preceding program is a demonstration for duplicate keys.

The predefined function and the predefined method for dictionary is tabulated in Table 8.1 and Table 8.2.

TABLE 8.1 Dictionary Functions

Function	Description
cmp(d1,d2)	Compares both elements of both dictionary
len(d)	Total length of the dictionary(d)
Str(d)	String representation of dictionary
Type(variable)	Return type of dictionary

TABLE 8.2 Dictionary Methods

Method	Description
Dict.clear	Removes all elements of dictionary
Dict.copy	Shallow copy of dictionary
Dict.fromKeys()	Creates a new dictionary with keys from seq and values *set* to *value*
Dict.get(key,default=None)	For *key* key, returns value or default if key not in dictionary
Dict.has_key(key)	Returns *true* if key in dictionary *dict, false* otherwise
Dict.items()	Returns a list of *dicts* (key, value) tuple pairs
Dict.keys()	Returns list of dictionary dict's keys
Dict.setdefault(key,default=None)	Similar to get() but will set dict[key]=default if *key* is not already in dict
Dict.update(d2)	Adds dictionary *dict2*'s key values pairs to *dict*
Dict.values()	Returns list of dictionary *dicts* values

Program: Creating dictionary

```
d={1:"this",2:"is",3:"to",4:"test"}
print(d)
d1=dict(a="this",b="is",c="to",d="test")
print(d1)
```

Output

```
{1: 'this', 2: 'is', 3: 'to', 4: 'test'}
{'a': 'this', 'b': 'is', 'c': 'to', 'd': 'test'}
```

Program: creating dictionaries by using from keys ()

```
k=('k1','k2','k3')
v=(10,20,30)
```

```
d=dict.fromkeys(k,v)
print(d)
V1=(10)
d1=dict.fromkeys(k,v1)
print(d1)
d2=dict.fromkeys(k)
print(d2)
```

Output

```
{'k1': (10, 20, 30), 'k2': (10, 20, 30), 'k3': (10,
  20, 30)} {'k1': 10, 'k2': 10, 'k3': 10}
{'k1': None, 'k2': None, 'k3': None}
```

8.1 ACCESSING THE ELEMENTS OF THE DICTIONARY

- By using for loop
- By using the key as the index
- By using dictionaryname.values()
- By using dictionaryname.keys()
- By using dictionaryname.items()

Program

```
d={1:"this",2:"is",3:to",4:"test"}
print(d)
for x in d:
print("key:",x,"value:",d.get(x))
print("using index")
for x in d:
print(d[x])
print("keys")
for x in d.values():
print(x)
print("values")
for x in d.keys():
print(x)
print("items")
for x,y in d.items():
print(x,y)
```

Output

```
{1: 'this', 2: 'is', 3: 'to', 4: 'test'}
key: 1 value: this
key: 2 value: is
key: 3 value: to
key: 4 value: test
using index
this
is
to
test
keys
this
is
to
test
values
1
2
3
4
items
1 this
2 is
3 to
4 test
```

Program

```
d={1:"this",2:"is",3:"to",4:"test"}
k=d.keys()
print(k)
v=d.values()
print(v)
x=d.items()
print(x)
```

Output

```
dict_keys([1, 2, 3, 4])
dict_values(['this', 'is', 'to', 'test'])
dict_items([(1, 'this'), (2, 'is'), (3, 'to') (4,
 'test')])
```

The preceding program prints the dictionary keys and values separately.

Program: Dictionary sorting

```
d={3:"to",2:"is",1: "this",4:"test"}
print("origianal",d)
print("sorting keys",sorted(d.keys()))
print("sorted dictionary:",sorted(d.items()))
print("sorted reverse dictionary:",
sorted(d.items(),reverse=True))
```

Output

```
origianal {3: 'to', 2: 'is', 1: 'this', 4: 'test'}
sorting keys [1, 2, 3, 4]
sorted dictionary: [(1, 'this'), (2, 'is'), (3, 'to'),
  (4, 'test')]
sorted reverse dictionary: [(4, 'test'), (3, 'to'),
  (2, 'is'), (1, 'this')]
```

8.2 COPYING THE DICTIONARY

There are two ways to copy the dictionary

- By using copy ()

- By using = operator

Program

```
d={1:"this",2:"is",3:"to",4:"test"}
print(d)
d1=d.copy()
print(d1)
d2=dict(d)
print(d2)
```

Output

```
{1: 'this', 2: 'is', 3: 'to', 4: 'test'}
{1: 'this', 2: 'is', 3: 'to', 4: 'test'}
{1: 'this', 2: 'is', 3: 'to', 4: 'test'}
```

The preceding program copies the dictionary using copy ().

Program

```
d={1:"this",2:"is",3:"to",4:"test"}
print(d)
d1=d
print("copy d1:",d1)
d2=dict(d)
print("copy uisng dict():",d2)
```

Output

```
{1: 'this', 2: 'is', 3: 'to', 4: 'test'}
copy d1: {1: 'this', 2: 'is', 3: 'to', 4: 'test'}
copy uisng dict(): {1: 'this', 2: 'is', 3: 'to', 4:
  'test'}
```

The preceding program performs dictionary copy using = operator.

8.3 NESTED DICTIONARY

A dictionary that consists of another dictionary is called the nested dictionary.

Program

```
d={'a': 'this', 'b': 'is', 'c': 'to', 'd': 'test'}
d1={'a1': 'this', 'b1': 'is', 'c1': 'to', 'd1':
  'test'}
d2={"d": d, "d1":d1}
print(d2)
```

Output

```
{'d': {'a': 'this', 'b': 'is', 'c': 'to', 'd':
  'test'}, 'd1': {'a1': 'this', 'b1': 'is', 'c1':
  'to', 'd1': 'test'}}
```

The previous section is an example for the nested dictionary.

Program

```
d={'a': 'python', 'b': ["this","is","to","test"]}
print(d)
```

Output

```
{'a': 'python', 'b': ['this', 'is', 'to', 'test']}
```

The preceding program consists of a list as the dictionary element.

Program

```
d={'a': 'python', 'b': tuple(("this","is","to","test")),
'c':set(("this is to test")),'d':frozenset(("this","is
 ","to","test"))}
print(d)
```

Output

```
{'a': 'python', 'b': ('this', 'is', 'to', 'test'),
 'c': {'o', 'i', 't', 'h', 's', ", 'e'}, 'd':
 frozenset({'test', 'is', 'to', 'this'})}
```

The preceding program consists of three data types to the Python dictionary.

8.4 CHANGING THE DICTIONARY VALUES

There are two ways to change the values of the dictionary:

- By using the key as the index

- By using the update ()

Program

```
d={1:"this",2:"is",3:"to",4:"test"}
print("orginal",d)
d[4]="testing"
print("modified",d)
d.update({4:"test dictionary"})
print("updated",d)
```

Output

```
orginal {1: 'this', 2: 'is', 3: 'to', 4: 'test'}
modified {1: 'this', 2: 'is', 3: 'to', 4: 'testing'}
updated {1: 'this', 2: 'is', 3: 'to', 4: 'test
 dictionary'}
```

The preceding program is modifying and updating dictionary.

8.5 ADDING THE ELEMENTS TO THE DICTIONARY

There are two ways in Python to add elements to the existing dictionary:

- By using the key as the index
- By using the update ()

Program

```
d={1:"this",2:"is",3:"to",4:"test"}
print(d)
d["test"]=1
print(d)
```

Output

```
{1: 'this', 2: 'is', 3: 'to', 4: 'test'}
{1: 'this', 2: 'is', 3: 'to', 4: 'test', 'test': 1}
```

The preceding program adds elements to dictionary by using key as the index.

Program

```
d={1:"this",2:"is",3:"to",4:"test"}
print("orginal",d)
d.update({5:"python",6:"dictionary"})
print("updated",d)
```

Output

```
orginal {1: 'this', 2: 'is', 3: 'to', 4: 'test'}
updated {1: 'this', 2: 'is', 3: 'to', 4: 'test', 5:
  'python', 6: 'dictionary'}
```

The preceding program adds elements to the dictionary using the update().

8.6 REMOVING THE ELEMENTS OF THE DICTIONARY

There are four ways to delete the elements of the dictionary in Python:

- By using pop () – removes the item of the specified key

- By using pop item () – removes the last inserted element
- By using del keyword – removes the element by using key as the index
- By using clear () – empties the dictionary

Program

```
d={1:"this",2:"is",3:"to",4:"test"}
print(d)
print(d.popitem())
print(d)
d.pop(1)
print(d)
del d[3]
print(d)
```

Output

```
{1: 'this', 2: 'is', 3: 'to', 4: 'test'}
(4, 'test')
{1: 'this', 2: 'is', 3: 'to'}
{2: 'is', 3: 'to'}
{2: 'is'}
```

The preceding program removes elements from dictionary.

Program

```
d={1:"this",2:"is",3:"to",4:"test"}
print(d)
d.clear()
print(d)
```

Output

```
{1: 'this', 2: 'is', 3: 'to', 4: 'test'}
{}
```

The preceding program clears the elements of the dictionary.

8.7 DICTIONARY COMPREHENSION

Dictionary comprehension is a technique of transforming a dictionary to another dictionary.

Program

```
d={i.lower(): i.upper() for i in 'python'}
print(d)
```

Output

```
{'p': 'P', 'y': 'Y', 't': 'T', 'h': 'H', 'o': 'O',
   'n': 'N'}
```

The preceding program performs dictionary comprehension using string methods.

Program

```
d={i: i*i for i in range(5)}
print(d)
s="python"
d1={i: s[i] for i in range(0,len(s))}
print(d1)
d2={i:i*i for i in [1,2,3,4,5]}#uisng list
print(d2)
d3={i:i*i for i in (1,2,3,4,5)}#uisng tuple
print(d3)
d4={i:i*i for i in {1,2,3,4,5}}
print(d4)
d5={x:i for x,i in enumerate(["this","is","to","test"])}
print(d5)
```

Output

```
{0: 0, 1: 1, 2: 4, 3: 9, 4: 16}
{0: 'p', 1: 'y', 2: 't', 3: 'h', 4: 'o', 5: 'n'}
{1: 1, 2: 4, 3: 9, 4: 16, 5: 25}
{1: 1, 2: 4, 3: 9, 4: 16, 5: 25}
{1: 1, 2: 4, 3: 9, 4: 16, 5: 25}
{0: 'this', 1: 'is', 2: 'to', 3: 'test'}
```

The preceding program creates dictionaries using dictionary comprehension of different data types.

Program

```
d={i: i for i in range(20) if i%2==0}
print("even elements dictionary",d)
```

Output

```
even elements dictionary {0: 0, 2: 2, 4: 4, 6: 6, 8:
  8, 10: 10,12: 12,14: 14,16: 16,18: 18}
```

The preceding program accesses even elements from the dictionary using dictionary comprehension.

Program

```
d={1:"this",2:"is",3:"to",4:"test"}
print("original",d)
d1={k:v for(k,v) in d.items()}
print("copy",d1)
d2={k*2:v for(k,v) in d.items()}
print("copy d2",d2)
d3={k:v*2 for(k,v) in d.items()}
print("copy d3",d3)
d4={k:v.capitalize() for(k,v) in d.items()}
print("copy",d4)
```

Output

```
original {1: 'this', 2: 'is', 3: 'to', 4: 'test'}
copy {1: 'this', 2: 'is', 3: 'to', 4: 'test'}
copy d2 {2: 'this', 4: 'is', 6: 'to', 8: 'test'}
copy d3 {1: 'thisthis', 2: 'isis', 3: 'toto', 4:
  'testtest'}
copy {1: 'This', 2: 'Is', 3: 'To', 4: 'Test'}
```

The preceding program performs dictionary copy using dictionary comprehension.

Program

```
d={1:'a',1.5:'b',True:'c',(0,1):'d'}
print(d)
```

Output

```
{1: 'c', 1.5: 'b', (0, 1): 'd'}
```

The preceding program creates dictionary with different data types as keys.

8.8 OPERATORS IN DICTIONARY

We can use the different operators to perform some operations in the dictionary. Some examples are listed here.

Program

```
d={1:"this",2:"is",3:"to",4:"test"}
print(d)
print("1 in d:",1 in d)
print ("test in d:","test" in d.values())
print("5 not in d:",5 not in d)
```

Output

```
{1: 'this', 2: 'is', 3: 'to', 4: 'test'}
1 in d: True
test in d: True
5 not in d: True
```

The preceding program uses the membership operators on dictionary.

Program

```
d={1:"this",2:"is",3:"to",4:"test"} d1={1:"this",2:
  "is",3:"to",4:"test",
5:"pyhton",6:"dictionary"}
print("d:",d)
print("d1:",d1)
print("d==d1:",d==d1)
print("d!=d1:",d!=1)
```

Output

```
d: {1: 'this', 2: 'is', 3: 'to', 4: 'test'}
d1: {1: 'this', 2: 'is'. 3: 'to' 4: 'test', 5:
  'pyhton', 6: 'dictionary'}
d==d1: False
d!=d1: True
```

The preceding program uses the equality operators on dictionary.

EXERCISE

1. Concatenate two dictionaries.

2. Create a dictionary where the keys are the numbers.

3. Sum all the values in the dictionary.

4. Sort a dictionary based on the keys.

5. Find the max value in the dictionary.

6. Print the dictionary in the table form.

7. Split the dictionary into two lists.

## CHAPTER 9

Modules and Packages

A module cab defines functions, classes, and variables. A module is a container that consists of functions. When a module is imported, its content is implicitly executed by Python. The initialization takes place only once, when the first import occurs on the assignments done by the module aren't repeated unnecessarily.

9.1 PYTHON IMPORT STATEMENT

The user can use any python source file as a module by implementing an import statement in some other python source file.

Syntax: Import module name

If there is a need to import more than one module, instead of using more than one import statement, list all the modules in a single import statement, and all the modules are separated by commas.

```
import module1[, module2[, module3 . . . module N]]
```

9.2 PYTHON FROM . . . IMPORT STATEMENT

Pythons from statement lets the programmer import particular attributes from a module into the existing namespace. The statement from import does not import all the complete module in the current namespace.

DOI: 10.1201/9781003414322-9

Syntax

```
from module-name import attribute2[, attribute2 . . .
  attribute n]]
```

To import all names from a module into the current name space, use import *.

Syntax

```
from module import *
```

Namespace

A namespace is a space.

Note: The names in a single namespace should be unique.

A package in Python is a directory structure, and it consists of modules, sub-packages, and sub-sub-packages.

Modules are files containing Python statements and definitions like functions and class definitions.

Module

Program: Invoking parameter less function using module

```
[54] %%writefile sample1.py
     def fun1():
             print("this is to test module")

     Writing sample1.py

[55] import sample1
     sample1.fun1()

     this is to test module
```

In the preceding program, fun1() exists in module sample1.py. In the main program, the first line is the import sample1, that is, we are importing the module sample1, and after importing the module, we can use all the variables and the functions from the imported module. The second line of the main program is the sample1.fun1(). This is a valid statement because we have imported the module sample1, and we are invoking the function fun1() from the module sample1. The output for this program is this is to test module.

Program

```
[56]   %%writefile sample2.py
       def square(n):
                print("square",n*n)
       def cube(n):
                print("cube",n*n*n)

Writing sample2.py

[57]   import sample2
       sample2.square(10)
       sample2.cube(5)

       square 100
       cube 125
```

The preceding program is about invoking parameterized function using module. The module name is the sample2. In sample2, module square and cube are two different functions. In the second program, we are importing the sample2 module, so we can use the square and the cube functions directly. The program outputs the square and cube values.

Program

```
       %%writefile sample3.py
       class samp:
           def display(self):
                print("display method")

Writing sample3.py

[63]   import sample3 as t
       s=t.samp()
       s.display()

       display method
```

The preceding program is invoking non-parameterized function using module. The module name is the sample3. In sample3 module display is a user-defined function. In the second program we are importing the sample3 module as t, and s is the object for the class samp that was created in the module sample3. By using this object we can invoke the class function that existed in another module.

Program

```
[64]    %%writefile sample4.py
        class testing:
                def display(self):
                        print("display method")
  Writing sample4.py
[65]    from sample4 import *
        s=testing()
        s.display()
display method
```

The preceding program is invoking non-parameterized function using module. The module name is the sample4. In sample4 module display is a user-defined function. In the second program we are importing the sample4 module. Here see the difference, in the previous programs we used only statement import module name, but here from module import * means importing all classes form the specified module. Next created the object for the class testing that was created in the module sample4. By using this object we can invoke the class function that existed in another module.

Program

```
[66]    %%writefile mymodule.py
        class testing1:
            def __init__(self,i,j):
                print("constructor")
                self.i=i
                self.j=j
            def display(self):
                print("i=",self.i)
                print("j=",self.j)

        Writing mymodule1.py

        from mymodule1 import *
        s=testing1(10,20)
        s.display()

        constructor
        i= 10
        j= 20
```

The preceding program is invoking parameterized constructor and parameterized function using module. The module name is the mymodule. In mymodule display is a user-defined function. In the second program we are importing the mymodule. Next created the object for the class testing1 that was created in the module mymodule. At the time of the object creation, the constructor of the class automatically invokes s. By using this object we can invoke the class function that existed in another module.

Program

```
[68]  %%writefile mymodule1.py
      class sample:
              def __init__(self,i,j):
                      print("constructor")
                      self.i=i
                      self.j=j
              def display(self):
                      print("i=",self.i)
                      print("j=",self.j)

  Writing mymodule1.py

[69]  from mymodule1 import *
      s=sample(10,20)
      s.display()
      print("in main prg i=",s.i)

      constructor
      i= 10
      j= 20
      in main prg i= 10
```

The preceding program is invoking parameterized constructor and non-parameterized function using module. The module name is the mymodule1. In mymodule1 display is a user-defined function. In the second program we are importing the mymodule1. Next created the object for the class sample that was created in the module mymodule1. At the time of the object creation, the constructor of the class automatically invokes. By using this object, we can invoke the class function that existed in another module. In the main program, the variables of the class that existed in another module was invoked and retrieved the value of those variables.

Program

```
[70]  %%writefile mymodule2.py
      class sample:
              def __init__(self,i,j) :
                      print("constructor")
                      self.i=i
                      self.j=j
              def display(self):
                      print("i=",self.i)
                      print("j=",self.j)

      Writing mymodule2.py

[71]  from mymodule2 import *
      S=sample(10,20)
      s.display()
      s.i=100
      print("in main prg i=",s.i)

      constructor
      i= 10
      j= 20
      in main prg i= 100
```

The preceding program is invoking parameterized constructor and non-parameterized function using module. The module name is the mymodule2. The mymodule2 display is a user-defined function. In the second program we are importing the mymodule2. Next created the object for the class sample that was created in the module mymodule2. At the time of the object creation, the constructor of the class automatically invokes. By using this object, we can invoke the class function that existed in another module. In the main program, the variables of the class that existed in another module was invoked and retrieved the value of those variables. Here changing the module variable in main class.

Program

```
[72]  %%writefile mymodule3.py
      class sample:
```

```
            def __init__(self,i,j):
                    print("sample constructor")
                    self.i=i
                    self.j=j
            def display(self):
                    print("i=",self.i)
                    print("j=",self.j)
    class test:
            def __init__(self,s):
                    print("test constructor")
                    self.s=s
            def put(self):
                    print("string:",self.s)

    Writing mymodule3.py

[73]   from mymodule3 import *
       s=sample(10,20)
       s.display()
       s.i=100
       print("in main prg i=",s.i)
       t=test("python")
       t.put()
       t.s="module example"
       print("in main prg i=",t.s)

       sample constructor
       i= 10
       j= 20
in main prg i= 100
       test constructor
       string: python
       in main prg i= module example
```

The preceding program is invoking parameterized constructor and non-parameterized function of the multiple classes using module. The module name is the mymodule3. In mymodule3, two different classes called the sample and test were created. The user-defined functions display and put are functions in the classes sample, and in the second program we are importing the mymodule3. Next created the object for the class sample and test that was created in the module mymodule3. At the time of the object creation, the constructor of the class automatically invokes. By using this object, we can invoke the class function that existed in another module. In the main program, the variables of the class that existed in another module was invoked and retrieved the value of those variables.

Program: Printing the functions in the module

```
%%writefile mymodule5.py
class samplee:
        def __init__(self,i,j):
                print("sample constructor")
                self.i=i
                self.j=j
        def display(self):
                print("i=",self.i)
                print("j=",self.j)
    class testt:
        def __init__(self,s):
                print("test constructor")
                self.s=s
        def put(self):
                print("string:",self.s)
    def fun1():
            print("parameterless function")
    def square(n):
            print("square",n*n)
    def cube(n):
            print("cube",n*n*n)

    from mymodule5 import *
    print(dir(mymodule5))
    s=samplee(10,20)
    s.display()
    s.i=150
    s.j=s.i*3
    print("in main prg i=,j=",s.i,s.j)
    t=testt("test class")
    t.put()

    t.s="usharani"
    print("in main prg i=",t.s)
    mymodule5.fun1()
    mymodule5.square(5)
    mymodule5.cube(5)
```

Output

```
['__builtins__', '__cached__', '__doc__', '__file__',
'__loader__', '__name__', '__package__', '__spec__',
'cube', 'fun1', 'samplee', 'square', 'testt']
Sample constructor
i= 10
j= 20
in main prg i=,j= 150 450
test constructor
string: test class
in main prg i= usharani
parameterless function
square 25
cube 125
```

The preceding program is invoking parameterized constructor and non-parameterized function of the multiple classes and non-class functions using module.

9.3 PACKAGE

A package in Python is a collection of one or more relevant modules.

Program

Step 1: Mounted the GDrive in colab

```
[11]        from google.colab import drive
            drive.mount('/content/GDrive/')

            Mounted at /content/GDrive/

[13]        import os
            print (os.listdir('GDrive'))

            ['MyDrive', '.shortcut-targets-by-id',
'.file-revisions-by-id', '.Trash-0']
```

Step 2: Created pythonpackage and change the path to the created packages

```
[15]        path = "GDrive/MyDrive/pythonpackage"
            os.mkdir(path)

[16]        os.chdir('GDrive/MyDrive/pythonpackage')
```

Step 3: Create file p1.py in package pythonpackage

```
[17]        %%writefile p1.py
            def fun1():

                        print("this is p1.py function")
            Writing p1.py
```

Step 4: Create file p22.py in package pythonpackage

```
[55]        %%writefile p22.py
            def fun2():
                        print("this is p2.py function")

            Writing p22.py
```

```
[46]        %cd'/content/GDrive/My Drive/pythonpackage'

            /content
```

```
 ▶          !ls
```

```
 ▷          p1.py   p2.py   __pycache__
```

Step 5: Imported the pythonpackage and the p1 file and call the function fun1 that was created in the file p1

```
[48]        import p1
            from p1 import *
            p1.fun1()

            this is p1.py function
```

Step 6: Imported the p2 file and call the function fun2 that was created in the file p22

```
            import p22
            from p22 import *
            p22.fun2()

            this is p2.py function
```

Program

Step 1: Mounted the GDrive in colab

```
[11]        from google.colab import drive
            drive.mount('/content/GDrive/')

            Mounted at /content/GDrive/

[13]        import os
            print (os.listdir('GDrive'))

            ['MyDrive', '.shortcut-targets-by-id',
'.file-revisions-by-id', '.Trash-0']
```

Step 2: Created pythonpackage and change the path to the created packages

```
[15]        path = "GDrive/MyDrive/pythonpackage"
            os.mkdir(path)

[16]        os.chdir('GDrive/MyDrive/pythonpackage')
```

Step 3: Created file p3.py in package pythonpackage

```
%%writefile p3.py
class sample:
        def __init__(self,i,j):
                print("sample constructor")
                self.i=i
                self.j=j
        def display(self):
                print("i=",self.i)
                print("j=",self.j)
```

Step 4: Created file p4.py in package pythonpackage

```
%%writefile p4.py
class test:
        def __init__(self,s):
                print("test constructor")
                self.s=s
        def put(self):
                print("string:",self.s)
```

Step 5: Imported the p3 module, its variables, and methods and imported the p4 module, its variables, and methods

```
import p3
from p3 import *
import p4
from p4 import *
s=sample(10,20)
s.display()
s.i=100
s.j=s.i*3
print("in main prg i=,j=",s.i,s.j)
t=test("python")
t.put()
t.s="package example"
print("in main prg s=",t.s)
```

Output

```
Sample constructor
i= 10
j= 20
in main prg i=,j= 100 300
test constructor
string: python
in main prg i= package example
```

The preceding program created classes in the files and store in the package my_package

Program

p5.py
```
def f3():
print("testing outside colab function")
[93]     from google.colab import files
         src = list(files.upload().values())[0]
         open('mylib.py','wb').write(src)
         import mylib
         mylib.f3()
         Choose Files p5.py
•        p5.py(n/a) - 53 bytes, last modified:
9/11/2021 - 100% done
```

```
saving p5.py to p5 (22).py
testing outside colab function
```

The preceding program is importing the Python file at run time and loading that file function at run time. The uploaded file name is p5.py. It is saved in the local desktop directory and uploaded at run time.

EXERCISE

1. Retrieve the elements of the list in the module program.

2. Retrieve the elements of the dictionary in the module program.

3. Retrieve the elements of the tuple and set in the module program.

4. Print the multiplication table using the module concept.

5. Display the contents of the CSV file using the module concept.

## CHAPTER 10

Functions

A function is a part of reusable code and provides a better modularity. Functions can have parameters and return values. The functions in Python are of four types:

- Built-in functions – Python language supports predefined functions like print (), input ().

- Predefined functions – The programmers can create their own functions.

- Modules

- Lambda functions

10.1 DEFINING A FUNCTION

Guidelines to define a function in Python:

1. Function blocks start with the keyword **def** followed by the user-defined function name and parentheses.

2. The input parameters or arguments should be put within these parentheses.

3. The parentheses are followed by the colon (:).

4. The initial statement of a function is the documentation string or doc string of the function, and this statement is the optional.

DOI: 10.1201/9781003414322-10

5. The statements in the function are indented.

6. The last statement of the function is the return statement. This state-ment exists the function and this statement is the optional.

7. Function ends where the nesting or indent ends.

Syntax of Function

```
def function name([parameters]):
#Doc string
Statement-1
Statement-2
Statement-3
return[expression]
```

Example Program

```
def test ():
print ("this is inside the function")
print ("this is the second statement inside the
function")
test()
```

The output for the preceding program is as follows:

```
this is inside the function
this is the second statement inside the function
```

Note: The variable name and the function name should not be the name.

For example:

```
def test ():
print ("inside function")
test="a"
test()
```

Output

```
----------------------------------------------------------------
TypeError                              Traceback (most
recent call last)
```

```
<ipython-input-98-4b4c6e06c695> in <module>()
2 print ("inside function")
3 test="a"
---->4 test()
TypeError: 'str' object is not callable
------------------------------------------------------------
```

Type error has occurred in the preceding program because the variable name and the function name are the same – test is given for both the variable and function.

Note: Name Error exception will be thrown if we invoke a function before defining it.

For example:
```
test () #calling a function before defining the function
test ()
def test ():
print("inside function")
```

Output

```
------------------------------------------------------------
TypeError                        Traceback (most
recent call last)
<ipython-input-100-a2dea2f337e3> in <module>()
---->1 test () #calling a function before defining the
function test ()
2 def test ():
3      print("inside function")
TypeError: 'str' object is not callable
```

The name error has occurred in the preceding program because the function test is calling in line 1 before it is defined. The error name 'test' is not defined has occurred.

There is no limitation for the number of the parameters in the function. At the time of calling the function, the first argument is copied to the first parameter, the second argument is copied to the second parameter, and the process continues for the rest of the arguments.

Program

```
def sum (i, j):
print ("sum=", i+ j)
sum (10,20)
```

Output

```
sum= 30
```

The program is about function with two parameters. In the preceding program the value 10 is copied to the parameter i, and the value 20 is copied to the parameter j. The previous section is an example for the positional parameters.

Program

```
def sum (i, j, k):
print ("sum=", i+ j+ k)
sum (10,20,30)
```

Output

```
sum= 60
```

The program is about function with three parameters. In the preceding program the value 10 is copied to the parameter i, the value 20 is copied to the parameter j, and the value 30 is copied to the parameter k. The previous section is an example for the positional parameters.

10.2 PASS BY REFERENCE

All the parameters or the arguments in the python are passed by reference. When the programmer changes the passed value in the function, the change echoes in the calling function.

Program

```
def test():
global 1
print(1)
1= [2,3,4,5]
1= [0,1]
```

```
test()
print("in main list=",1)
```

Output

```
[0, 1]
in main list= [2, 3, 4, 5]
```

In the preceding program the list elements have been modified, and its new values are reflected back in main function.

10.3 FUNCTION ARGUMENTS

Parameter is a variable, and it exists only inside functions in which they have been defined. Assigning a value to the parameter is done at the time of the function invocation. Parameters and arguments are different. Parameters live inside functions, whereas arguments exist outside the function. Parameter is an ordinary variable inside the function, and these parameters aren't visible anywhere else except inside the function body.

Note: The programmer must provide as many arguments as there are provided parameters; otherwise error will occur.

For example
```
def test (i, j):
print("i=", i, "j=",j)
def(10)
```

Output

```
File "<ipython-input-105-4ec7275e726b>", line 3
def(10)
   ^

SyntaxError: invalid syntax
```

Error has occurred in the preceding program because at the time of calling the function test, only one argument was given, but at the function definition, two parameters were given. The arguments and the parameters should be the same for the same function.

The programmer can call a function by applying the following types of formal arguments:

1. Required arguments

2. Keyword arguments

3. Default arguments

4. Variable arguments

10.3.1 Required Arguments

The required arguments are also called the positional arguments. The number of the arguments in the function call would match accurately with the function definition. Required arguments are the arguments passed to a function in correct positional order, that is, the ith argument is copied to the ith parameter.

Program

```
def test(i,j):
print("i=",i,"j=",j)
test(10,20)
test(20,10)
```

Output

```
i= 10 j= 20
i= 20 j= 10
```

The preceding program is about positional arguments. At line 3 when function is called, the value 10 is passed to i, while calling second time test function, the value 20 is copied to the variable i.

10.3.2 Keyword Arguments

Keyword arguments are associated with the function calls. When the programmer uses the keyword arguments in a function call, the function definition recognizes the arguments by the parameter name. The programmer can skip the arguments or place them out of order as the python interpreter is able to utilize the keywords required to match the values with parameters. The position doesn't matter, that is, each arguments value knows its destination based on the name (key) used.

Program

```
def test(name,surname):
print("name:",name,"surname:",surname)
test(name="usharani",surname="bhimavarapu")
test(surname="bhimavarapu",name="usharani")
```

Output

```
name: usharani surname: bhimavarapu
name: usharani surname: bhimavarapu
```

Note: When mixing both the keyword and the positional parameters, the positional parameters should be before the keyword parameters.

Program

```
def add(a,b,c):
print("add=",(a+b+c))
add(10,c=20,b=30)
```

Output

```
add= 60
```

The preceding program is about mix of both the positional and the keyword arguments.

Program

```
def add(a,b,c):
print("add=",(a+b+c))
add(c=10,20,b=30)
```

Output

```
File "<ipython-input-110-f7d678c0b9db>", line 3
add(c=10,20,b=30)
   ^
SyntaxError: positional argument follows keyword
  argument
```

In the preceding program, an error has occurred because the first argument is the keyword argument, but the second argument is the positional argument, so syntax error has occurred. The positional arguments should be before the keyword arguments. Replace line 3 with add (c=20, a=20,b=30) and given in the next example.

Program

```
def add(a,b,c):
print("add=",(a+b+c))
add(c=10,a=20,b=30)
```

Output

```
add= 60
```

Program

```
def add(a,b,c):
print("add=",(a+b+c))
add(10,a=20,b=30)
```

Output

```
----------------------------------------------------------------
TypeError                         Traceback (most
recent call last)
<ipython-input-112-d05b0f077928> in <module>()
1 def add(a,b,c):
2  print("add=",(a+b+c))
---->3 add(10,a=20,b=30)

TypeError: add() got multiple values for argument 'a'
```

In the preceding program, in function call add (), the first argument is positional argument, and it is copied to the parameter a. The second argument is the keyword argument and trying to copy the value 20 again to the parameter a. The error has occurred at this point because of trying to pass multiple values to the same parameter a. When using keyword arguments, avoid passing more than one value to one parameter.

10.3.3 Default Arguments

A default argument is an argument that supposes a default value if a value is not given in the function call for that argument.

Program

```
def add(a=1,b=5,c=8):
print("add=",(a+b+c))
add(10)
```

Output

```
add=   23
```

Program

```
def add(a=1,b=5,c=8):
print("add=",(a+b+c))
add(10,20,30)
```

Output

```
add=   60
```

Program

```
def add(a=1,b=5,c=8):
print("add=",(a+b+c))
add()
```

Output

```
add=   14
```

Program

```
def add(a=1,b=5,c=8):
print("add=",(a+b+c))
add(b=10)
```

Output

```
add=   19
```

Program

```
def add(a=1,b=5,c=8):
print("add=",(a+b+c))
add(a=10,c=20)
```

Output

```
add=   35
```

Program

```
def add(a,b=5,c):
print("add=",(a+b+c))
add(a=10,c=20)
```

Output

```
File "<ipython-input-118-957033311ea7>", line 1
def add(a,b=5,c):
                 ^
SyntaxError: non-default argument follows default
  argument
```

When the user specifies the default arguments before the non-default argument, an error will arise.

 Note: The default arguments come after non-default arguments.

10.3.4 Variable Length Arguments

An asterisk (*) is arranged prior to the variable name that retains the values of all non-keyword arguments.

Program

```
def test(*args):
n = args[0]
for i in args:
if i < n:
n = i
return n

test(4,1,2,3,4)
```

Output

```
1
```

10.4 ANONYMOUS FUNCTIONS

The anonymous functions are not stated in the normal approach by using the def keyword. For the anonymous functions, the programmer must use the lambda keyword.

Syntax

```
lambda [arg1[, arg2[, arg3 . . . argn]]]: expression
lambda arguments: expression
```

Program

```
t=lambda: None
print(t)
```

Output

```
<function <lambda> at 0x7f301ff33d40>
```

The preceding program is for lambda statement.

Program

```
j = lambda i : i + 5
print(j(3))
```

Output

```
8
```

The preceding program is for lambda statement with one parameter.

Program

```
m = lambda i,j : i+j
print(m(3,4))
```

Output

```
7
```

The preceding program is for lambda statement with two parameters.

Program

```
s = [1,2,3,4,5,6,7]
m = list(map(lambda i: i + 2, s))
print(m)
```

Output

```
[3, 4, 5, 6, 7, 8, 9]
```

The preceding program is for lambda and the map ().

Program

```
s = [1,2,3,4,5,6,7]
m = list(filter(lambda i: i%2==0, s))
print(m)
```

Output

```
[2, 4, 6]
```

The preceding program is for lambda and the filter ().

10.5 RETURN STATEMENT

Return is a keyword in Python. The return statement is the last statement, and the return statement exists the function. The return statement is the optional statement. It may or may not contain the arguments. There are two variants for return statement.

Syntax

```
return
return(expression)
```

The return statement stops the function execution and goes back to the point of the function invocation. When the programmer wants to return to point of function invocation despite reaching the end of the program, they can use the variants of the return statement.

Program

```
def test():
    print("inside function")
```

```
return;
print("end of functions")
print("in main")
test()
print("end of main")
```

Output

```
in main
inside function
end of main
```

In the preceding program, despite reaching the end of the program, return to main program – unconditional return.

Program

```
def test():
return None
test()
print("end of main")
```

Output

```
end of main
```

The preceding program explicitly returning none in the user-defined function test.

 Note: Return implicitly means return None.

Program

```
def test(i):
 if(i<10):
print(" should be >10")
return
test(5)
print("end of main")
```

Output

```
should be >10
end of main
```

In the preceding program, the return is used in the conditional statement if.s.

Program

```
def test(i,j):
return(i+j)
print("add",test(5,10))
print("end of main")
```

Output

```
add 15
end of main
```

The preceding program result returns from the function.

Program

```
def test(i):
if(i<10):
   return True
print(test(5))
```

Output

```
True
```

The preceding program returns boolean values. If the value of variable(i) is less than value 10, then the program returns boolena value True.

10.6 FUNCTION VARIABLE SCOPE

Variables that are specified within a function body have a local extent, and the variables defined outside have a global scope. The variables declared inside the function body can be retrieved only in that function, whereas the global variables can be accessed throughout the program, that is, in all the functions.

Program

```
def test():
s="test"
print(s)
```

Output

```
python
```

Program

```
s="test"
def test():
s="python"
print(s)
print(s)
```

Output

```
test
```

Program

```
def test():
z=10
print("z=",z)
print("z=",z)
```

Output

```
------------------------------------------------------------
NameError                         Traceback (most
recent call last)
<ipython-input-144-4bf440b1933a> in <module>()
2 z=10
3 print("z=",z)
---->4 print("z=",z)

NameError: name '7' is not defined
```

Name error has occurred because the scope of the parameter is in the function itself. At line 4, trying to print the function parameter outside the function. So the error x not defined is raised.

Note: The parameters cannot be accessed outside the function.

Program

```
def test(x):
i=10
```

```
i*=x
print("inside function i=",i)
i=25
test(5)
print("in main i=",i)
```

Output

```
inside function i= 50
in main i= 25
```

Program

```
def test():
print("inside function i=",i)
i=10
test()
print("in main i=",i)
```

Output

```
inside function i= 10
in main i= 10
```

The preceding program accesses variable in function that is defined outside function.

Note: The functions variable shadows the outside program variable. A variable outside the function has a scope inside the function also.

Program

```
def test():
print("inside function i=",i)
i=i+1
i=10
test()
print("in main i=",i)
```

Output

```
--------------------------------------------------------------
UnboundLocalError        Traceback (most recent call
last)
```

```
<ipython-input-130-78236c23d9d2> in <module>()
3 i=i+1
4 i=10
----> 5 test()
6 print("in main i=",i)

<ipython-input-130-78236c23d9d2> in test()
1 def test():
----> 2      print("inside function i=",1)
3 i=i+1
4 i=10
5 test()
UnboundLocalError: local variable 'i' referenced
  before assignment
```

In the preceding program, an error occurred because the function is not able to modify the variable defined outside the function. In the cited example, the variable i is defined outside the function at line 4. As the variable i is defined outside the function, try to modify the variable i at line 3 inside the function. So the occur raised. This type of error can be removed by extending the scope of the variable. Without passing the argument, try to modify the variable that is out of the scope variable.

Program

```
def test(i):
print("inside function i=",i)
i+=1
i=10
test(i)
print("in main i=",i)
```

Output

```
inside function i= 10
in main i= 10
```

Modifications inside the function cannot reflect outside the function, that is, changing the parameter values does not reflect outside the function. The scope of the variable can be extended by using the global keyword.

Note: Scope of a variable can be extended inside the function by using the global keyword.

Program

```
def test():
global i
print("inside function i=",i)
i=i+1
i=10
test()
print("in main i=",i)
```

Output

```
inside function i= 10
in main i= 11
```

By using the global keyword inside the function, despite creating the new variable inside the function, the function uses the outside function defined variable. In the preceding program, using the global i at line 2, it makes the variable i global. At line 4, trying to modify the variable i, this modification reflects to the outside function.

Program

```
a=10
def test():
global a
print("inside function a=",a)
a=50
print("in main a=",a)
```

Output

```
in main a= 10
```

10.7 PASSING LIST TO FUNCTION

List can be sent as an argument to the function.

Program

```
def test(1):
```

```
for i in 1:
print(i)
1=["this","is","to","test"]
test(1)
```

Output

```
this
is
to
test
```

The preceding program accesses the list elements inside the function.

Program

```
def test():
global 1
print(1)
1=[2,3]
1=[0,1]
test()
print("in main list=",1)
```

Output

```
[0, 1]
in main list= [2, 3]
```

The preceding program modifies the list elements inside the function.

Program

```
def test():
global 1
print(1)
1=[2,3,4,5]
1=[0,1]
test()
print("in main list=",1)
```

Output

```
[0, 1]
in main list= [2, 3, 4, 5]
```

The preceding program appends the list elements inside the function.

Program

```
def test():
global 1
print(1)
del 1[1]
1=[0,1]
test()
print("in main list=",1)
```

Output

```
[0, 1]
in main list= [0]
```

The preceding program deletes list elements inside the function.

10.8 RETURNING LIST FROM THE FUNCTION

To return multiple values from the Python, we can return either the list or tuple.

Program

```
def test():
1=[]
print ("enter how many strings do u want to enter")
n=int(input())
for i in range(0,n,1):
s=input("enter string")
1.insert(i,s)
return 1
print(test())
```

Output

```
enter how many strings do u want to enter
3
enter stringtesting
enter stringpython
enter stringsample
['testing', 'python', 'sample']
```

The preceding program returns list from the function.

Program

```
def test():
1=[]
print("enter how many float \
values do u want to enter")
n=int(input())
for i in range(0,n,1):
f=float(input("enter float"))
1.insert(i,f)
return 1
1=test()
print(1)
sum=0
for i in range(len(1)):
sum+=1[i]
print("sum=",sum)
```

Output

```
enter how many float values do u want to enter
3
enter float1.1
enter float2.2
enter float3.3
[1.1, 2.2, 3.3]
sum= 6.6
```

The preecding program returns list and processes the list.

10.9 RECURSION

A function calling itself is known as recursion.

Program

```
def rec(n):
if n == 1:
return n
else:
return n*rec(n-1)
n = 5
if n < 0:
print("no factorial for negative numbers")
```

```
elif n == 0:
print("The factorial of 0 is 1")
else:
print("The factorial of", n, "is", rec(n))
```

Output

```
The factorial of 5 is 120
```

The preceding program is about factorial number using recursion.

Program

```
def fib(n):
if n <= 1:
return n
else:
return(fib(n-1) + fib(n-2))
n = 8

if n <= 0:
print("enter a positive integer")
else:
print("Fibonacci sequence:")
for i in range(n):
print(fib(i))
```

Output

```
Fibonacci sequence:
0
1
1
2
3
5
8
13
```

The preceding program is about finocchi series using recursion.

Program

```
def prime(i,n):
if n==i:
return 0
else:
if(n%i==0):
return 1
else:
return prime(i+1,n)
n=9
print ("Prime Number are: ")
for i in range(2,n+1):
if(prime(2,i)==0):
print(i,end=" ")
```

Output

```
Prime Number are:
2 3 5 7
```

The preceding program is about prime number series using recursion.

EXERCISE

1. Check the output for the following Python program:

   def test():

   print("inside function")

   test("1")

2. Check the output for the following Python program:

   test("1")

   def test():

   print("inside function")

   test()

3. Check the output for the following Python program:

```
def test():
print("inside function")
print("main function")
test()
print("end of main")
```

4. Check the output for the following program:

```
def test(name):
print("welcome",name)
name=input("enter ur name")
test(name)
```

5. Check the output for the following program:

```
def test(i):
print("inside function i=",i)
i=i+1
i=int(input("Enter integer:"))
print("in main i=",i)
test(i)
print("after function calling i=",i)
```

6. Check the result for the following Python program:

```
def test(name,surname):
print("name:",name,"surname:",surname)
test("usharani","bhimavarapu")
test("bhimavarapu","usharani")
```

7. Check the output for the following program:

```
def test():
i=10
print(i)
```

## CHAPTER 11

Date and Time

THE TIME MODULE AND the calendar module in Python helps to retrieve data and time. The time module has the predefined methods to represent the time and to process the time. The time are expressed in seconds since 00:00:00 hours January 1, 1970.

11.1 TIME MODULE

To access the time-related function, the user must import the time module.

Syntax

```
import time
```

Example

```
import time
t=time.time()
print(t)
```

Output

```
1631509053.0120902
```

The cited example prints ticks from January 1, 1970.

DOI: 10.1201/9781003414322-11

Example

```
import time
lt=time.localtime(time.time())
print(lt)
```

Output

```
time.struct_time(tm_year=2021, tm_mon=9, tm_mday=13,
tm_hour=4, tm_min=45, tm_sec=30, tm_wday=0,
tm_yday=256, tm_isdst=0)
```

The cited example prints local time.

11.2 CALENDAR

The calendar module has predefined methods to retrieve and process the year and month.

Example

```
import calendar
C=calendar.month(2020,10)
print(c)
```

Output

```
       October                  2020
Mo      Tu      We      Th      Fr      Sa      Su
                         1       2       3       4
 5       5       7       8       9      10      11
12      13      14      15      16      17      18
19      20      21      22      23      24      25
26      27      28      29      30      31
```

The cited example displays the calendar for the month 10 (October) and for the year 2020.

11.3 TIME MODULE

The time module has predefined methods and attributes to retrieve and process the time. The predefined attributes and the predefined methods of the time module is tabulated in Table 10.1 and Table 10.2.

TABLE 10.1   Predefined Attributes in Python Time Module

Attribute	Description
time.timezone	It is the offset of the local time zone from UTC in seconds.
Time.tzname	It is the pair of local dependent string.

TABLE 10.2   Methods in Time Module

Function	Description
time.altzone	It is the offset of local time zone to UTC in seconds.
time asctime ([tupletime])	Returns the date in a readable 24-character string.
time.clock()	Returns the current CPU time.
time.ctime()	Returns the date in a readable 24-character string in terms of seconds.
time.gmtime([secs])	Returns a time tuple of UTC time.
time.localtime([secs])	Returns the local time.
time.mktime(tupletime)	Returns the time since the epoch.
time.sleep(secs)	Suspends the calling thread for the specified time in terms of seconds.
time.strftime(fmt[,tupletime])	Returns the string format of time.
time.strptime (str,fmt='%a%b%d%H: %M:%S%Y')	Returns the time in the time tuple format.
time.time()	Returns the current time.
time.tzset()	Resets the time conversion rules.

11.4 CALENDAR MODULE

The calendar module has predefined methods to retrieve and process the year and month. By default, calendar considers the first day of the week as the Monday and last day of the week as Sunday. Calendar module provides the following list of functions.

The predefined methods in the calendar module are tabulated in Table 10.3. The date format codes are tabulated in Table 10.4.

TABLE 10.3   Predefined Methods in the Calendar Modules

Function	Description
calendar. calendar(year,w=2,l=1,c=6)	Returns calendar for year and formatted by the specified c, w and l.
calendar. firstweekday()	Returns the starting day of each week.
calendar. leapdays(y1,y2)	Returns the number of leap days between the given specified years.

(*Continued*)

TABLE 10.3 (*Continued*) Predefined Methods in the Calendar Modules

Function	Description
calendar. month (year,month,w=2,l=1)	Returns the calendar for specified month/
calendar. month calendar(year. month)	Returns a list of weeks.
calendar. month range(year. month)	Returns the weekday of the month and the total number of days in the specified month.
calendar.prcal(year,w=2,l=1,c=6)	Displays the calendar.
calendar.prmonth(year,month,w=2,l=1)	Displays the calendar for month.
Calendar. setfirstweekday(weekday)	Sets the weekday code. Default weekday codes are 0 to Monday and 6 to Sunday. Sets the weekday code.
Calendar. timegm(tupletime)	Returns the time in term of seconds.
Calendar. weekday(year, month,day)	Returns the weekday code for the specified date.
calendar. isleap(year)	Checks whether the specified year is leap or not.

TABLE 10.4 Date Format Codes

Directive	Meaning	Example
%a	Weekday abbreviated name	Sun, Mon,
%A	Weekday full name	Sunday, Monday, . . .
%w	Weekday in terms of decimal number	0, 1, 2, 3, 4, 5, 6
%d	Day of the month	01, 02, , 31
%b	Month abbreviated name	Jan, Feb
%B	Month full name	January, February, . . .
%m	Month in decimal form	01, 02, 012
%y	Year in decimal padded number (two digit)	00, 01, 099
%Y	Year as a decimal number (four digit)	0001, 002, . . . 2021, . . . 9999
%H	Hour (24) in decimal number	01, 02, . . . 023
%l	Hour(12) in decimal number	01, 02, . . . 012
%p	Time in the form of PM or AM	PM or AM
%M	Minutes	00, 01, . . . 059
%S	seconds	00, 01, . . . 059
%f	microsecond	000000, 000001, . . .
%z	HHMMSS form	
%Z	Time zone name	
%j	Day of the year in decimal number	001,002, . . . 366
%U	Weekday of the year in the decimal number (Sunday is the first day of the week)	00, 01, . . . 53

(*Continued*)

TABLE 10.4 (*Continued*) Date Format Codes

Directive	Meaning	Example
%W	Weekday of the year in the decimal number (Monday is the first day of the week)	00, 01, ... 53
%c	Local date and time	Mon Sep 13, 10:10:00
%x	Local date	13/09/2021
%X	Local time	10:10:00

11.5 THE DATETIME MODULE

The datetime module works with dates and times.

Syntax

import datetime

Getting the current date by using the datetime module is as follows:

```
import datatime
d = datetime.date.today()
print(d)
```

Output

```
2021-09-29
```

The today() method in the date class is used to get the date object, which contains the current local date.

11.6 THE PYTZ MODULE

The pytz module supports the datetime conversion, enables the time zone calculations, and allows to create the time zone–related datetime objects.

Example

```
import pytz
print('the timezones are', pytz.all_timezones, '\n')
```

The cited example returns all the time zones.

Example

```
import pytz
import datetime
from datetime import datetime
```

```
u = pytz.uzc
k = pytz.timezone('Asia/Kolkata')
print('UTC Time =', datetime.now(tz=u))
print('Asia Time =', datetime.now(tz=k))
```

Output

```
UTC Time = 2021-09-29 04:15:09.099077+00:00
Asia Time = 2021-09-29 09:45:09.100941+05:30
```

In the cited example, datetime instances were created using the time zone instance.

11.7 THE DATEUTIL MODULE

The dateutil module allows one to modify the dates and times.

```
from datetime import *
from dateutil.relativedelta import *
import calendar
NOW = datetime. now()
# Next month
print(NOW + relativedelta(months=+1))
 # Next month, plus one week
print(NOW + relativedelta(months=+1, weeks=+1))
 # Next month, plus one week, at 5 PM
Print(NOW + relativedelta(months=+1, weeks=+1,
hour=17))
```

Output

```
2021-10-29 04:29:08.289926
2021-11-05 04:29:08.289926
2021-11-05 17:29:08.289926
```

The cited example computes the relative dates for next week or next month.

Example

```
import calendar as c
print(c.month(2020,11))
```

Output

```
          November              2020
Mo        Tu        We        Th        Fr        Sa        Su
                                                             1
 2         3         4         5         6         7         8
 9        10        11        12        13        14        15
16        17        18        19        20        21        22
23        24        25        26        27        28        29
30
```

The cited example prints a specified month calendar in a specific year.

Example

```
import calendar as c
print(c.leapdays(1920,2020))
```

Output

```
25
```

The cited example prints count the leap years between the range of years.

Example

```
from datetime import date
print(date.today())
```

Output

```
2021-09-13
```

The cited example prints today's date.

Example

```
import calendar as c
print(c.calendar(2020,1,1,1))
```

Output

```
                              2020
         January               February                March
Mo Tu We Th Fr Sa Su  Mo Tu We Th Fr Sa Su  Mo Tu We Th Fr Sa Su
          1  2  3  4  5               1  2               1
 6  7  8  9 10 11 12   3  4  5  6  7  8  9   2  3  4  5  6  7  8
13 14 15 16 17 18 19  10 11 12 13 14 15 16   9 10 11 12 13 14 15
20 21 22 23 24 25 26  17 18 19 20 21 22 23  16 17 18 19 20 21 22
27 28 29 30 31           24 25 26 27 28 29     23 24 25 26 27 28 29
                                              30 31
          April                  May                   June
Mo Tu We Th Fr Sa Su  Mo Tu We Th Fr Sa Su  Mo Tu We Th Fr Sa Su
          1  2  3  4  5               1  2  3 1  2  3  4  5  6  7
 5  7  8  9 10 11 12   4  5  6  7  8  9 10 8   9 10 11 12 13 14
13 14 15 16 17 18 19  11 12 13 14 15 16 17 15 16 17 18 19 20 21
20 21 22 23 24 25 26  18 19 20 21 22 23 24 22 23 24 25 26 27 28
27 28 29 30              25 26 27 28 29 30 31 29 30
          July                 August               September
Mo Tu We Th Fr Sa Su  Mo Tu We Th Fr Sa Su  Mo Tu We Th Fr Sa Su
          1  2  3  4  5               1  2      1  2  3  4  5  6
 5  7  8  9 10 11 12   3  4  5  6  7  8  9   7  8  9 10 11 12 13
13 14 15 16 17 18 19  10 11 12 13 14 15 16  14 15 16 17 18 19 20
20 21 22 23 24 25 26  17 IS 19 20 21 22 23  21 22 23 24 25 26 27
27 28 29 30 31           24 25 26 27 28 29 30 28 29 30
                         31
         October               November               December
Mo Tu We Th Fr Sa Su  Mo Tu We Th Fr Sa Su  Mo Tu We Th Fr Sa Su
          1  2  3  4               1      1  2  3  4  5  6
 5  6  7  8  9 10 11   2  3  4  5  6  7  8   7  8  9 10 11 12 13
12 13 14 15 16 17 18   9 10 11 12 13 14 15  14 15 16 17 18 19 20
19 20 21 22 23 24 25  16 17 IS 19 20 21 22  21 22 23 24 25 26 27
26 27 28 29 30 31        23 24 25 26 27 28 29 28 29 30 31
                         30
```

The cited example prints all months of a specific year.

Example

```python
from datetime import date
t=date.today()
print("day",t.day)
print("month",t.month)
print("year",t.year)
```

Output

```
day 13
month 9
year 2021
```

The cited example prints the individual date components.

Example

```
from datetime import date
t=date.today()
print("weekday:",t.weekday())
```

Output

```
Weekday: 0
```

The cited example prints the weekday.

Note: Monday:0 . . . Sunday:7

Example

```
from datetime import datetime
print("Todays date and time:",datetime.now())
```

Output

```
Todays date and time: 2021-09-13 04:50:10.232992
```

The cited example prints today's date and time.

Example

```
from datetime import datetime
n=datetime.now()
print("weekday date and time:",m.strftime("%c"))
print("date" n.strftime("%x"))
print("Time:",n.strftime("%X"))
print("Hours and Minutes:",n.strftime("%H:%M"))
print("time with Meridie",n. strftime("%I:%M:%S %p"))
```

Output

```
weekday date and time: Mon Sep 13 04:50:23 2021
date 09/13/21
Time: 04:50:23
Hours and Minutes: 04:50
time with Meridie 04:50:23 AM
```

The cited example prints date and time using strftime formats.

Example

```
from datetime import date
d1=date(2019,11,19)
d2=date(2020,11,17)
d=d2-d1
print(d.days)
print(type(d))
```

Output

```
364
<class 'datetime.timedelta'>
```

The cited example prints difference between two dates.

Example

```
from datetime import date t=datetime.now()
print("Year 4 digits:",t.strftime("%Y")) print("Year 2
digits:",t.strftime("%y"))
print("Month:",t.strftime("%m"))
print("Minutes:",t.strftime("%M")) print("Date",t.
strftime("%d")) print("weekday",t.strftime("%a"))
print("weekday Fullname",t.strftime("%A"))
print("weekday(decimal)",t.strftime("%w"))
print("Month(abbr)",t.strftime("%b"))
print("Month(FullName)",t.strftime("%B"))
print("Microseconds:",t.strftime("%f"))
```

Output

```
Year 4 digits: 2021
Year 2 digits: 21
```

```
Month: 09
Minutes: 50
Date 13
weekday Mon
weekday Fullname Monday
weekday(decimal) 1
Month(abbr) Sep
Month(FullName) September
Microseconds: 270905
```

The cited example prints formatted data and time using strftime.

Example

```
import datetime
print("Max year",datetime.MAXYEAR)
print("Min Year",datetime.MINYEAR)
print(type(datetime.MAXYEAR)) print(type(datetime.
MINYEAR))
```

Output

```
Max year 9999
Min Year 1
<class 'int'>
<class 'int'>
```

The cited example prints the min and max year using the datetime module.

Example

```
import datetime
print("Min year",datetime.date.min)
print("Min year",datetime.date.max)
print(type(datetime.date.min))
print(type(datetime.date.max))
```

Output

```
Min year 0001-01-01
Min year 9999-12-31
<class 'datetime.date'>
<class 'datetime.date'>
```

The cited example prints the data of the min and max year using the datetime module.

Example

```
import datetime
d=datetime.date(2020,11,17)
print("year:",d.year)
print("month:",d.month)
print("day:",d.day)
```

Output

```
year: 2020
month: 11
day: 17
```

The cited example separates the date, month, and year of the given date.

Example

```
import datetime as d
n=d.date.today()
print(n)
n=n.replace(month=5,year=2021)
print(n)
```

Output

```
2021-09-13
2021-05-13
```

The cited example replaces today's date with the specified date.

Example

```
import datetime
d=datetime.date.today()
print(d.timetuple())
```

Output

```
time.struct_time(tm_year=2020, tm_mon=11, tm_mday=17,
tm_hour=0, tm_min=0, tm_sec=0, tm_wday=1, tm_yday=322,
tm_isdst=-1)
```

The cited example prints the time tuple attributes.

Example

```
import time
print(time.time())
```

Output

```
1605595205.6687665
```

The cited example prints the timestamp.

Example

```
import calendar as c
from datetime import date
t=date.today()
cal=c.Calendar()
y=t.year
m=t.month
print(cal.monthdays2calendar(y,m))
```

Output

```
[[(0, 0), (0, 1), (0, 2), (0, 3), (0, 4), (0, 5), (1, 6)],
[(2, 0), (3, 1), (4, 2), (5, 3), (6, 4), (7, 5), (8, 6)],
[(9, 0), (10, 1), (11, 2), (12, 3), (13, 4), (14, 5), (15,
6)], [(16, 0), (17, 1), (18, 2), (19, 3), (20, 4), (21, 5),
(22, 6)], [(23, 0), (24, 1), (25, 2), (26, 3), (27, 4),
(28, 5), (29, 6)], [(30, 0), (0, 1), (0, 2), (0, 3), (0,
4), (0, 5), (0, 6)]]
```

The cited example demonstrates monthdays2calendar ().

Example

```
import calendar as c
from datetime import date
t=date.today()
cal=c .Caleindar()
y=t.year
m=t.month
```

```
for i in cal.monthdays2calendar(y,m):
print(i)
```

Output

```
[(0, 0), (0, 1), (0, 2), (0, 3), (0, 4), (0, 5), (1, 6)]
[(2, 0), (3, 1), (4, 2), (5, 3), (6, 4), (7, 5), (8, 6)]
[(9, 0), (10, 1), (11, 2), (12, 3), (13, 4), (14, 5), (15, 6)]
[(16, 0), (17, 1), (18, 2), (19, 3), (20, 4), (21, 5), (22, 6)]
[(23, 0), (24, 1), (25, 2), (26, 3), (27, 4), (28, 5), (29, 6)]
[(30, 0), (0, 1), (0, 2), (0, 3), (0, 4), (0, 5), (0, 6)]
```

The cited example demonstrates monthdays2calendar ().

Example

```
import calendar as c
from datetime import date
t=date.today()
y=t.year
m=t.month
c= calendar.TextCalendar(firstweekday=5)
print(c.formatmonth(y,m,w= 5))
```

Output

```
              September      2021
Sat     Sun     Mon     Tue     Wed     Thu     Fri
                                1       2       3
 4       5       6       7       8       9      10
11      12      13      14      15      16      17
18      19      20      21      22      23      24
25      26      27      28      29      30
```

The cited example demonstrates monthdays2calendar ().

Example

```
import calendar as c
from datetime import date t=date.today()
y=t.year
m=t.month
c= calendar.TextCalendar(firstweekday=1)
print(c.formatmonth(y,m,w=3))
```

Output

```
           September 2021
Tue        Wed        Thu        Fri        Sat        Sun        Mon
            1          2          3          4          5          6
7           8          9         10         11         12         13
14         15         16         17         IS         19         20
21         22         23         24         25         26         27
28         29         30
```

The cited example demonstrates format month ().

Example

```
import calendar as c
from datetime import date
t=date.today()
y=t.year
m=t.month
cal=c.Calendar()
for i in cal.monthdayscalendar(y,m):
print(i)
```

Output

```
[0, 0, 1,       2,           3,           4, 5]
[6, 7, 8,       9,          10,          11,          12]
[13, 14,       15,          16,          17,          18,          19]
[20, 21,       22,          23,          24,          25,          26]
[27, 28,       29,          30,          0, 0         , 0]
```

The cited example demonstrates month days calendar ().

Example

```
import calendar as c
from datetime import date
t=date.today()
y=t.year
m=t.month
cal=c.Calendar()
print(cal.monthdayscalendar(y,m))
```

Output

```
[[0, 0, 0, 0, 0, 0, 1], [2, 3, 4, 5, 6, 7, 8], [9, 10,
11, 12, 13, 14, 15], [16, 17, 18, 19, 20, 21, 22],
[23, 24, 25, 26, 27, 28, 29], [30, 0, 0, 0, 0, 0, 0]]
```

The cited example demonstrates month days calendar().

Example

```python
import calendar as c
from datetime import date
t=date.today()
y=t.year
m=t.month
cal=c.Calendar()
for i in cal.itermonthdays2(y,m):
print(i, end=" ")
```

Output

```
(0, 0) (0, 1) (0, 2) (0, 3) (0, 4) (0, 5) (1, 6)
(2, 0) (3, 1) (4, 2) (5, 3) (6, 4) (7, 5) (8, 6)
(9, 0) (10, 1) (11, 2) (12, 3) (13, 4) (14, 5) (15,
6) (16, 0) (17, 1) (18, 2) (19, 3) (20, 4) (21, 5)
(22, 6) (23, 0) (24, 1) (25, 2) (26, 3) (27, 4)
(28, 5) (29, 6) (30, 0) (0, 1) (0, 2) (0, 3) (0, 4)
(0, 5) (0, 6)
```

The cited example iterates month days calendar ().

Example

```python
import calendar as c
from datetime import date
t=date.today()
cal=c.Calendar(firstweekday=5)
y=t.year
m=t.month
for i in cal.itermonthdays2(y,m):
print(i, end=" ")
```

Output

```
(0, 5) (1, 6) (2, 0) (3, 1) (4, 2) (5, 3) (6, 4) (7,
5) (8, 6) (9, 0) (10, 1) (11, 2) (12, 3) (13, 4) (14,
5) (15, 6) (16, 0) (17, 1) (18, 2) (19, 3) (20, 4)
(21, 5) (22, 6) (23, 0) (24, 1) (25, 2) (26, 3) (27,
4) (28, 5) (29, 6) (30, 0) (0, 1) (0, 2) (0, 3) (0, 4)
```

The cited example demonstrates month days calendar ().

Example

```
import calendar as c
cal=c.Calendar()
for i in cal.iterweekdays():
print(i, end=" ")
```

Output

```
0 1 2 3 4 5 6
```

The cited example demonstrates weekdays calendar ().

Example

```
import calendar as c
cal=c.Calendar(firstweekday=5)
for i in cal.iterweekdays():
print(i, end=" ")
```

Output

```
5 6 0 1 2 3 4
```

The cited example retrieves the weekdays if the first day of the week is the 5.

Example

```
import calendar as c
from datetime import date
```

```
t=date.today()
cal=c.Calendar()
y=t.year
m=t.month
for day in cal.itermonthdays(y,m):
print(day,end=" ")
```

Output

```
0 0 0 0 0 0 1 2 3 4 5 6 7 8 9 10 11 12 13 14 15 16 17
18 19 20 21 22 23 24 25 26 27 28 29 30 0 0 0 0 0 0 0
```

The cited example retrieves the month days in the calendar.

Example

```
import calendar as c
from datetime import date
t=date.today()
cal=c.Calendar()
y=t.year
m=t.month
for i in cal.yeardayscalendar(y,m):
print(i)
```

Output

```
[[[0, 0, 1, 2, 3, 4, 5], [6, 7, 8, 9, 10, 11, 12],
[13, 14, 15, 16, 17, 18, 19], [20, 21, 22, 23, 24, 25,
26], [27, 28, 29, 30, 31, 0, 0]], [[0, 0, 0, 0, 0, 1,
2], [3, 4, 5, 6, 7, 8, 9], [10, 11, 12, 13, 14, 15,
16], [17, 18, 19, 20, 21, 22, 23], [24, 25, 26, 27,
28, 29, 0]], [[0, 0, 0, 0, 0, 0, 1], [2, 3, 4, 5, 6,
7, 8], [9, 10, 11, 12, 13, 14, 15], [16, 17, 18, 19,
20, 21, 22], [23, 24, 25, 26, 27, 28, 29], [30, 31, 0,
0, 0, 0, 0]], [[0, 0, 1, 2, 3, 4, 5], [6, 7, 8, 9, 10,
11, 12], [13, 14, 15, 16, 17, 18, 19], [20, 21, 22,
23, 24, 25, 26], [27, 28, 29, 30, 0, 0, 0]], [[0, 0,
0, 0, 1, 2, 3], [4, 5, 6, 7, 8, 9, 10], [11, 12, 13,
14, 15, 16, 17], [18, 19, 20, 21, 22, 23, 24], [25,
26, 27, 28, 29, 30, 31]], [[1, 2, 3, 4, 5, 6, 7], [8,
9, 10, 11, 12, 13, 14], [15, 16, 17, 18, 19, 20, 21],
[22, 23, 24, 25, 26, 27, 28], [29, 30, 0, 0, 0, 0,
```

```
0]], [[0, 0, 1, 2, 3, 4, 5], [6, 7, 8, 9, 10, 11, 12],
[13, 14, 15, 16, 17, 18, 19], [20, 21, 22, 23, 24, 25,
26], [27, 28, 29, 30, 31, 0, 0]], [[0, 0, 0, 0, 0, 1,
2], [3, 4, 5, 6, 7, 8, 9], [10, 11, 12, 13, 14, 15,
16], [17, 18, 19, 20, 21, 22, 23], [24, 25, 26, 27,
28, 29, 30], [31, 0, 0, 0, 0, 0, 0]], [[0, 1, 2, 3, 4,
5, 6], [7, 8, 9, 10, 11, 12, 13], [14, 15, 16, 17, 18,
19, 20], [21, 22, 23, 24, 25, 26, 27], [28, 29, 30, 0,
0, 0, 0]], [[0, 0, 0, 1, 2, 3, 4], [5, 6, 7, 8, 9, 10,
11], [12, 13, 14, 15, 16, 17, 18], [19, 20, 21, 22,
23, 24, 25], [26, 27, 28, 29, 30, 31, 0]], [[0, 0, 0,
0, 0, 0, 1], [2, 3, 4, 5, 6, 7, 8], [9, 10, 11, 12,
13, 14, 15], [16, 17, 18, 19, 20, 21, 22], [23, 24,
25, 26, 27, 28, 29], [30, 0, 0, 0, 0, 0, 0]]]
[[[0, 1, 2, 3, 4, 5, 6], [7, 8, 9, 10, 11, 12, 13],
[14, 15, 16, 17, 18, 19, 20], [21, 22, 23, 24, 25, 26,
27], [28, 29, 30, 31, 0, 0, 0]]]
```

The cited example retrieves the month days in the calendar for the complete year.

Example

```
import calendar as c
from datetime import date
t=date.today()
cal=c.Calendar()
y=t.year
m=t.month
for i in cal.itermonthdates(y,m):
print(i,end=" ")
```

Output

```
2020-10-26 2020-10-27 2020-10-28 2020-10-29 2020-10-30
2020-10-31 2020-11-01 2020-11-02 2020-11-03 2020-11-04
2020-11-05 2020-11-06 2020-11-07 2020-11-08 2020-11-09
2020-11-10 2020-11-11 2020-11-12 2020-11-13 2020-11-14
2020-11-15 2020-11-16 2020-11-17 2020-11-18 2020-11-19
2020-11-20 2020-11-21 2020-11-22 2020-11-23 2020-11-24
2020-11-25 2020-11-26 2020-11-27 2020-11-28 2020-11-29
2020-11-30 2020-12-01 2020-12-02 2020-12-03 2020 12-04
2020-12-05 2020-12-06
```

The cited example retrieves the days of the month starting from today's date.

Example

```python
import calendar as c
from datetime import date
t=date.today()
y=t.year
m=t.month
cal= calendar.TextCalendar(firstweekday=1)
print(c.prmonth(y,m,w=3))
```

Output

```
        September 2021
Mon     Tue     Wed     Thu     Fri     Sat     Sun
                 1       2       3       4       5
  6       7       8       9      10      11      12
 13      14      15      16      17      18      19
 20      21      22      23      24      25      26
 27      28      29      30
None
```

Example

```python
import calendar as c
from datetime import date
t=date.today()
y=t.year
m=t.month
cal= calendar.TextCalendar()
print(cal.formatyear(y,2))
```

Output

```
                         2021

      January               February               March
Mo Tu We Th Fr Sa Su   Mo Tu We Th Fr Sa Su   Mo Tu We Th Fr Sa Su
             1  2  3     1  2  3  4  5  6  7     1  2  3  4  5  6  7
 4  5  6  7  8  9 10     8  9 10 11 12 13 14     8  9 10 11 12 13 14
11 12 13 14 15 16 17    15 16 17 18 19 20 21    15 16 17 18 19 20 21
18 19 20 21 22 23 24    22 23 24 25 26 27 28    22 23 24 25 26 27 28
25 25 27 28 29 30 31                            29 30 31
```

```
                         2021
      April                May               June
Mo Tu We Th Fr Sa Su  Mo Tu We Th Fr Sa Su  Mo Tu We Th Fr Sa Su
          1  2  3  4               1  2         1  2  3  4  5  6
 5  6  7  8  9 10 11   3  4  5  6  7  8  9   7   8  9 10 11 12 13
12 13 14 15 16 17 18  10 11 12 13 14 15 16  14 15 16 17 18 19 20
19 20 21 22 23 24 25  17 18 19 20 21 22 23  21 22 23 24 25 26 27
26 27 28 29 30        24 25 26 27 28 29 30  28 29 30
                      31
      July               August             September
Mo Tu We Th Fr Sa Su  Mo Tu We Th Fr Sa Su  Mo Tu We Th Fr Sa Su
          1  2  3  4                  1         1  2  3  4  5
 5  6  7  8  9 10 11   2  3  4  5  6  7  8    6  7  8  9 10 11 12
12 13 14 15 16 17 18   9  10 11 12 13 14 15  13 14 15 16 17 18 19
19 20 21 22 23 24 25  16 17 18 19 20 21 22  20 21 22 23 24 25 26
26 27 28 29 30 31     23 24 25 26 27 28 29  27 28 29 30
                      30 31
     October             November             December
Mo Tu We Th Fr Sa Su  Mo Tu We Th Fr Sa Su  Mo Tu We Th Fr Sa Su
             1  2  3   1  2  3  4  5  6  7         1  2  3  4  5
 4  5  6  7  8  9 10   8  9 10 11 12 13 14   6  7  8  9 10 11 12
11 12 13 14 15 16 17  15 16 17 18 19 20 21  13 14 15 16 17 18 19
18 19 20 21 22 23 24  22 23 24 25 26 27 28  20 21 22 23 24 25 26
25 25 27 28 29 30 31  29 30                 27 28 29 30 31
```

The preceding program displays the calendar for the complete year based on today's date and year.

Example

```
import calendar as c
print(c.firstweekday())
```

Output

```
0
```

The preceding program displays the first day of the week in the numerical form.

Example

```
from datetime import timedelta
t1 = timedelta(seconds = 15)
```

```
t2 = timedelta(seconds = 74)
t3 = t1 - t2
print("t3 =", t3)
print("t3 =", abs(t3))
```

Output

```
t3 = -1 day, 23:59:01
t3 = 0:00:59
```

The preceding program displays the negative delta time.

Example

```
from datetime import datetime, timedelta
now = datetime.now()
tomorrow = timedelta(days=+1)
print(now + tomorrow)
```

Output

```
2021-09-13 05:52:56.799161
2021-09-14 05:52:56.799161
```

The preceding program displays today's date and the next date using the time delta module.

Example

```
from datetime import datetime, timedelta
t1 = datetime.now()
t2 = timedelta(days=+1)
print(t1+t2)
```

Output

```
2021-09-14 06:52:01.829130
```

The preceding program performs arithmetic addition operation on time delta.

Example

```
from datetime import datetime, timedelta
t1 = datetime.now()
```

```
t2 = timedelta(days=+1)
print(t1-t2)
```

Output

```
2021-09-12 06:52:18.075289
```

The preceding program performs arithmetic subtraction operation on time delta.

Example

```
from datetime import timedelta
d = timedelta(microseconds=-1)
print(d*5)
```

Output

```
-1 day, 23:59:59.999995
```

The preceding program performs arithmetic multiplication operation on time delta.

Example

```
from datetime import timedelta
d = timedelta(microseconds=-100)
print(d*0.1)
```

Output

```
-1 day, 23:59:59.999990
```

The preceding program performs float multiplication operation on time delta.

Example

```
from datetime import datetime, timedelta
d = timedelta(microseconds=-100)
t2 = timedelta(days=+1)
print(d/t2)
```

Output

```
-1.157407407407074e-09
```

The preceding program performs arithmetic division operation on time delta.

Example

```
from datetime import datetime, timedelta
t2 = timedelta(days=+1)
print(t2/5)
```

Output

```
4:48:00
```

The preceding program performs arithmetic division operation on time delta.

Example:

```
from datetime import datetime, timedelta
t2 = timedelta(days=+1)
print(t2/0.5)
```

Output

```
2 days, 0:00:00
```

The preceding program performs float division operation on time delta.

Example

```
from datetime import datetime, timedelta
t1 = timedelta(microseconds=-100)
t2 = timedelta(days=+1)
print(t1%t2)
```

Output

```
23:59:59.999900
```

The preceding program performs modulo division operation on time delta.

Example

```
from datetime import datetime timedelta
tl = timedelta(microseconds=-100)
t2 = timedelta(days=+l)
q,r=divmod(tl,t2)
print(q)
print(r)
```

Output

```
-1
23:59:59.999900
```

The preceding program performs div mod operation on time delta.

Example

```
from datetime import datetime, timedelta
tl = timedelta(microseconds=-100)
t2 = timedelta(days=+l)
print(+tl)
print(-tl)
print(+t2)
print(-t2)
```

Output

```
-1 day, 23:59:59.999900
0:00:00.000100
1 day, 0:00:00
-1 day, 0:00:00
```

The preceding program performs unary addition and unary subtraction operation on time delta.

Example

```
from datetime import datetime, timedelta
tl = timedelta(microseconds=-100)
t2 = timedelta(days=+l)
print(str(tl))
print(str(t2))
```

Output

```
-1 day, 23:59:59.999900
1 day, 0:00:00
```

The preceding program performs the string representation of the time delta object.

Example

```
from datetime import datetime, timedelta
t1 = timedelta(microseconds=-100)
t2 = timedelta(days=+1)
print(repr(t1))
print(repr(t2))
```

Output

```
datetime.timedelta(days=-1, seconds=86399,
microseconds=999900)
datetime.timedelta(days=1)
```

The preceding program displays the representation of the time delta object.

EXERCISE

1. Print a particular weekday using relative delta ().

2. Print the previous month and previous week using relative delta.

3. Write a Python program to subtract three days from today's date.

4. Write a Python program to print today's date and the current time.

5. Write a Python program to print today's date and weekday.

6. Write a Python program to print today's date, yesterday's date, and tomorrow's date.

7. Write a Python program to print all the Saturdays of the specified year.

8. Write a Python program to print the delay of 5 minutes 15 seconds from the current time.

9. Write a Python program to print the five-column calendar of the specified year.

10. Write a Python program to find whether the current year is a leap year or not.

## CHAPTER 12

Regular Expression

A regex, or regular expression, is a sequence of characters that forms a search pattern. Regular expression can be used to check if a string contains the specified search pattern. Python has a built-in package called re, which can be used to work with the regular expressions. When the users import the re module, they can start using regular expressions. In Python re module supports regular expressions. The raw strings can be expressed as r'expression.

12.1 THE RE MODULE

Python supports the python regular expression functionality, and this functionality is supported using the re module. This module consists of the predefined attributes and the methods to perform the regular pattern matching and searching.

Syntax

```
import re
```

The different meta characters and different patterns are tabulated in Tables 12.1, 12.2, 12.3, and 12.4.

DOI: 10.1201/9781003414322-12

TABLE 12.1   Regular Expression Modifiers

Modifier	Description
re.l	Case-insensitive matching
re.L	By following the current system locale, interpretation of the words using the alphabetic group
re.M	Do search at the end of the line and at the beginning of the line
re.S	Checking for period match including the new line
re.U	Interprets the letters as per the Unicode letters
re.X	Ignores white space

TABLE 12.2   Regular Expression Patterns w.r.t Control Characters

Pattern	Description
^	Searches at the beginning of the line
$	Searches at the end of the line
.	checks the single character
[. . .]	Searches for the characters within the brackets
[^ . . .]	Searches for the characters not with in the brackets

TABLE 12.3   Regular Expression Patterns w.r.t Patttern Matching

Pattern	Description
re*	Searches for the zero or more occurrences of the specified pattern
re+	Searches for the one or more occurrences of the specified pattern
re?	Searches for the zero or one occurrences of the specified pattern
re{n}	Searches for the n number of occurrences of the specified pattern
re{n,}	Searches for the n or more occurrences of the specified pattern
re{n,m}	Searches at least n and at most m occurrences of the specified pattern
a|b	Searcher either for a or b
(re)	Remember the matched pattern
(?:re)	Does not remember the matched pattern
(?# . . .)	Comment
(?=re)	Specifies the position using the pattern
(?!re)	Specifies the position using the negation
(?>re)	Searches for the independent pattern

TABLE 12.4   Regular Expression Patterns w.r.t Escape Sequence

Pattern	Description
\w	Searches to match for word
\W	Searches to match for non-word
\s	Searches for the white space
\S	Searches for the non-white space
\d	Searches for the digits
\D	Searches for the non-digits
\A	Returns match pattern if the corresponding characters are at the beginning of the string.
\Z	Search at the end of the string
\z	Search at the end of the string
\G	Returns at the last match found
\b	Returns match pattern if the corresponding characters are at the beginning of the string or at the end of the string
\B	Returns match pattern if the corresponding characters are present in the string but not at the beginning of the string
\1 . . . \9	Returns a match for any digit between 0 and 9

12.2 PYTHON MATCH FUNCTION

The match is the predefined method in the re module, and this method matches the pattern with the string by using the optional flags.

Syntax

```
re.match(pattern,string,flags=0)
```

The parameters for the match function are as follows:

- **Pattern** – This sequence is the regular expression to be equated.
- **String** – This would be examined to match the pattern at the beginning of string.
- **Flags** – These are modifiers, and different modifiers are separated using bitwise or (|).

The match function yields match object on equal, otherwise none.

The group function () of match object

group(num=0) – returns complete match

groups () – returns all similar subgroups in a tuple

Example

```
import re
s="this is to test the python regular expressions"
m=re.match(r'(.*)are(.*?).*', s,re.M)
print(m)
if m:
print(m.group())
print(m.group(1))
print(m.group(2))
```

Output

```
None
```

Example

```
import re
s="this is to test"
x=re.match("^t . . .",s)
if x:
print("found")
else:
print("not found")
```

Output

```
found
```

The preceding program searches whether any word starts with 't' and word length is four.

12.3 THE SEARCH FUNCTIONS

The search function explores for first existence of re sequence within string.

Syntax

```
re.search(pattern,string,flags=0)
```

The parameters for the search function are as follows:

- Pattern – This pattern is to be matched.

- String – Searched at the beginning of string.

- Flags – These are modifiers, and different modifiers are separated using bitwise or (|). The flags in the search function are optional

The search function sends match object on success, otherwise none

The group function () of match object

group(num=0) – returns complete match

groups () – returns all similar subgroups in a tuple

Example: Search function

```
import re
txt = "It is still raining"
s = re.search("\s", txt)
print("First white-space at:", s.start())
```

Output

```
First white-space at: 2
```

In the preceding example the first occurrence of the first empty space is returned.

Example

```
import re
str = "This is to test"
s = re.search("test", str)
print(s.span())
print(s.group())
print(s.string)
```

Output

```
(11, 15)
test
This is to test
```

The preceding program searches for the string test in the given string str (i.e., This is to test).

Example

```
import re
str = "This is to test the regex test"
s = re.search("test", str)
print(s)
print(type(s))
```

Output

```
<re.Match object; span=(11, 15), match='test'>
<class 're.Match'>
```

Example

```
import re
s = "this is to test"
r = re.search(r"\bt", s)
print(r.start())
print(r.end())
print(r.span())
```

Output

```
0
1
(0, 1)
```

Example

```
import re
s = "this is to test"
r = re.search(r"\D{2} t", s)
print(r.group())
```

Output

```
is t
```

12.4 PYTHON MATCH FUNCTION VS SEARCH FUNCTION

Match function checks for a match only at the beginning of the string, whereas the search object checks for a match anywhere in the string.

Example

```
import re

a = ["this", "is", "to", "test"]
for s in a:
x = re.match("(g\w+)\W(g\w+)", s)
if x:
print((x.groups()))

a = ["this", "is", "to", "test"]
s = 'test'
for t in a:
print('Found "%s" in "%s" -> ' % (t, s), end=' ')
if re.search(t, s) :
print('found a match!')
else:
print('no match')
```

Output

```
Found "this" in "test" -> Found "is" in "test" ->
Found "to" in "test" -> Found "test" in "test" ->
found a match!
no match
```

Regular expression modifiers

Modifier	Description
re.I	Case-insensitive matching
re.L	By following the current system locale, interpretation of the words using the alphabetic group
re.M	Do search at the end of the line and at the beginning of the line.
re.S	checking for period match including the new line
re.U	Interprets the letters as per the Unicode letters.
re.X	Ignores white space

Regular expression patterns

Pattern	Description
^	Searches at the beginning of the line
$	Searches at the end of the line
.	checks the single character
[...]	Searches for the characters within the brackets
[^...]	Searches for the characters not with in the brackets
re*	Searches for the zero or more occurrences of the specified pattern
re+	Searches for the one or more occurrences of the specified pattern
re?	Searches for the zero or one occurrences of the specified pattern
re{n}	Searches for the n number of occurrences of the specified pattern
re{n,}	Searches for the n or more occurrences of the specified pattern
re{n,m}	Searches at least n and at most m occurrences of the specified pattern
a|b	Searcher either for a or b
(re)	Remember the matched pattern
(?:re)	Does not remember the matched pattern
(?#...)	comment
(?=re)	Specifies the position using the pattern
(?!re)	Specifies the position using the negation
(?>re)	Searches for the independent pattern
\w	Searches to match for word
\W	Searches to match for non-word
\s	Searches for the white space
\S	Searches for the non-white space
\d	Searches for the digits
\D	Searches for the non-digits
\A	Returns match pattern if the corresponding characters are at the beginning of the string.
\Z	Search at the end of the string
\z	Search at the end of the string
\G	returns at the last match found
\b	Returns match pattern if the corresponding characters are at the beginning of the string or at the end of the string.
\B	Returns match pattern if the corresponding characters are present in the string but not at the beginning of the string
\1..\9	Returns a match for any digit between 0 and 9

12.5 THE COMPILE FUNCTION

The compile function in the re module is used to compile the regular expression patterns. This function helps to look for the occurrences of the matched pattern in the specified string.

Syntax

```
re.compile(patern, flags=0)
```

The parameters for the compile function are as follows:

- Pattern – This pattern is to be matched.
- Flags – For flags, refer to Table 12.1.

The re.compile() returns the matched pattern.

Example

```
import re
x=re.compile('\w+')
Print(x.findall("This pen costs rs100/-"))
```

Output

```
['This', 'pen', 'costs', 'rs100']
```

The preceding example displays alphanumeric group characters.

Example

```
import re
x=re.compile('\d')
print(x.findall("this is my 1st experiment on regex"))
```

Output

```
['1']
```

The preceding program extracts the digits from the given string.

12.6 THE FINDALL () FUNCTION

The findall () function checks for all specified pattern matches in the given string.

Syntax

```
re.findall(patern,string, flags=0)
```

The parameters for the match function are as follows:

- **Pattern** – This sequence is the regular expression to be equated.

- **String** – This would be examined to match the pattern at the beginning of string.

- **Flags** – These are modifiers, and different modifiers are separated using bitwise or (|).

Example

```
import re
x=re.compile('\W')
print(x.findall("This is costs rs100/0-"))
```

Output

```
[' ', ' ', ' ', '/', '-']
```

The preceding program displays the non-alphanumeric characters.

Example

```
import re
x=re.compile('\d')
print(x.findall("we got independence on 15th
  august 1947"))
```

Output

```
['1', '5', '1', '9', '4', '7']
```

The preceding program extracts all the digits from the given string. The \d extracts all the digits.

Example

```
import re
x=re.compile('\d+')
print(x.findall("we got independence on 15th
  august 1947"))
```

Output

```
['15', '1947']
```

Example

```
import re
str = "This is to test the regex test"
s = re.findall("test", str)
print(s)
```

Output

```
['test', 'test']
```

12.7 THE SPLIT () FUNCTION

The Python re.split () function splits the given string based on the given specific pattern. This function returns the list, which consists of the resultant substring of the given string.

Syntax

```
re.split(pattern, string, maxsplit=0, flags=0)
```

The parameters for the match function are as follows:

- **Pattern** – This sequence is the regular expression to be equated.
- **String** – This would be examined to match the pattern at the beginning of string.
- **Maxsplit** – The maximum number of splits that the user wants to perform.
- **Flags** – These are modifiers, and different modifiers are separated using bitwise or (|).

Example

```
import re
s = 'five:5 twenty one:21 ten:10'
p = '\d+'
r=re.split(p, s, 1)
print(r)
```

Output

```
['five:', ' twenty one:21 ten:10']
```

Example

```
from re import split
print(split('\W+', 'this, is,to, test'))
print(split('\W+', 'This, is,to, test'))
print(split('\W+', 'This is my 1st experiment in re'))
print(split('\d+', 'This is my 100 experiment in re'))
```

Output

```
['this', 'is', 'to', 'test']
['This', 'is', 'to', 'test']
['This', 'is', 'my', '1st', 'experiment', 'in', 're']
['This is my ', 'experiment in re']
```

Example

```
import re
print(re.split('\d+', 'this is 1 test', 1))
print(re.split('[a-f]+', 'This IS To Test', flags=re.
  IGNORECASE))
print(re.split('[a-f]+', 'This IS To Test'))
```

12.8 THE SUB () FUNCTION

The Python re.sub () function replaces the occurrences of the specified pattern with the target pattern in the given string.

Syntax

```
re.sub(pattern, repl, string, count=0, flags=0)
```

The parameters for the match function are as follows:

- **Pattern** – This sequence is the regular expression to be equated.

- **Repl** – Replace string.

- **String** – This would be examined to match the pattern at the beginning of string.

- **Count** – Number of replacements.

- **Flags** – These are modifiers, and different modifiers are separated using bitwise or (|).

Example

```
import re
s = 'this is to test'
p = '\s+'
r=''
s1 = re.sub(p, r, s)
print(s1)
```

Output

```
thisistotest
```

Example

```
import re
s = 'this is to test'
r=''
s1 = re.sub(r'\s+', r, s, 1)
print(s1)
```

Output

```
thisis to test
```

Example

```
import re
s = 'this is to test'
p = '\s+'
r=''
s1 = re.subn(p, r, s)
print(s1)
```

Output

```
('thisistotest', 3)
```

Output

```
['this is ', ' test']
['This IS To T', 'st']
['This IS To T', 'st']
```

12.9 THE RE.ESCAPE () FUNCTION

Python automatically escapes all the metacharacter by using the escape () function.

Example

```
import re
print(re.escape("this is to test"))
print(re.escape("this is to test \t ^test"))
```

Output

```
this\ is\ to\ test
this\ is\ to\ test\ \          \ \^test
```

Example

```
import re
expr = '(a^b)'
eqn = 'f*(a^b) - 3*(a^b)'
re.sub(re.escape(expr) + r'\Z', 'c', eqn)
```

Output

```
'f*(a^b) - 3*c'
```

EXERCISE

1. Print a string that has 'b' followed by zero or one 'a'.

2. Find sequences of uppercase letter followed by underscore.

3. Find sequences of uppercase letter followed by lowercase letters.

4. Extract the words that matches a word containing 's'.

5. Extract the words that start with a number or a underscore.

6. Extract the words that end with a number.

7. Extract all the substring from the given string.

8. Print the occurrences and the position of the substring within the string.

9. Replace all occurrences of space with a comma.

10. Extract all five-character words from the given string.

Index